moneyzen

ALSO BY MANISHA THAKOR
(WITH COAUTHOR SHARON KEDAR)

On My Own Two Feet: A Modern Girl's Guide to Personal Finance

Get Financially Naked: How to Talk Money with Your Honey

moneyzen

THE SECRET TO FINDING YOUR "ENOUGH"

Manisha Thakor
with Lisa Sweetingham

HARPER
BUSINESS

An Imprint of HarperCollins*Publishers*

MONEYZEN. Copyright © 2023 by Manisha Thakor. All rights reserved. Printed in the United States of America. No part of this book may be used or reproduced in any manner whatsoever without written permission except in the case of brief quotations embodied in critical articles and reviews. For information, address HarperCollins Publishers, 195 Broadway, New York, NY 10007.

HarperCollins books may be purchased for educational, business, or sales promotional use. For information, please email the Special Markets Department at SPsales@harpercollins.com.

FIRST EDITION

Designed by Kyle O'Brien

Library of Congress Cataloging-in-Publication Data
Names: Thakor, Manisha, author.
Title: Moneyzen / Manisha Thakor with Lisa Sweetingham.
Includes bibliographical references.
Identifiers: LCCN 2022058481 (print) | LCCN 2022058482 (ebook) | ISBN 9780063247963 (hardcover) | ISBN 9780063247970 (ebook)
Subjects: LCSH: Finance, Personal. | Finance—Psychological aspects.
Classification: LCC HG179 .T438 2023 (print) | LCC HG179 (ebook) | DDC 332.024–dc23/eng/20221209
LC record available at https://lccn.loc.gov/2022058481
LC ebook record available at https://lccn.loc.gov/2022058482

23 24 25 26 27 LBC 5 4 3 2 1

*This book is dedicated to all who have struggled
with feelings of Never Enough.*

You are not alone. There is life beyond the hustle. You are enough.

CONTENTS

moneyzen

———

If my experience is any guide, there are two paths to becoming part of a cult. One is a conscious decision. The other is a series of small, consistent, unconscious steps toward the flickering flame. Looking back, I can't say I wasn't warned.

It started in 1992, when I was a senior at Wellesley College, and I was offered a highly coveted job in a two-year financial analyst training program of a global investment bank based in London. The firm was starting to build its U.S. presence, and I was excited to be hired into their New York City mergers-and-acquisitions group. In those days, a post-undergraduate job at a prestigious Wall Street firm like this could put you on the fast track to getting into a top-tier business school and on the path to making the kind of money I could only dream about.

My training began in London, where I was housed in an expensive flat in Kensington, one of the chicest parts of town. Night after night, my cohorts and I were wined and dined at London's best restaurants by senior members of the firm who introduced us to the organization and its culture. It was a glamorous time for a girl from a small, midwestern town.

After six weeks of training, I was sent to the New York office to begin work. In contrast to my heady time in London, the everyday culture here was classic Wall Street: intense, relentless, and exhausting. Young investment banking analysts like me mostly sat around all day, waiting for a managing director to dump a pile of work on our desks at about 5 p.m., which we would then sweat over until three or four in the morning. We were constantly trying to outdo one another: Who could handle the largest volume of work? Who could curry favor with the most powerful members of the deal teams?

Competition was not limited to new recruits; the senior executives were also engaged in their own *Game of Thrones*–like battle to advance their careers, resulting in their need to squeeze as much support work out of us as possible. At least once or twice a week, they squeezed so hard that we were forced to pull all-nighters to get it all done. Bleary-eyed as the sun began to rise, we'd freshen up in the bathroom and drink copious amounts of coffee to wake us up before the senior members of the team began to file in at 7:30 a.m.

After six months, I'd had enough. No longer willing to work in an environment that felt like a mixed-martial-arts cage fight, I decided to quit. My plan was to get into business school and then pivot my career toward an area of finance called investment management, a sector that was worlds apart in terms of culture. From what I could tell, investment management had a vibe that felt less like a death match and more like the world of professional tennis—competitive and demanding, yet in a civilized setting.

After all the time and expense the company had invested in my London training, I was sure my bosses would be furious that I was leaving the two-year program early. I steeled myself for the recriminations sure to come. To my surprise, they never did. Instead, the executive managing director to whom I submitted my resignation responded wistfully: "We'll miss you, Manisha, but good for you. Get out before you have a family and they get so used to the kind of money and lifestyle this brings that you *can't* get out." It almost felt as if I were escaping some kind of cult.

In fact, as word of my leaving trickled out, two additional, highly respected executives each brought me into their offices, shut their doors, and bid me farewell with nearly identical sentiments. They both said it with such a mix of bitterness and resignation, that I can still hear their prescient warnings today: *Get out while you can.*

Unfortunately, I never did "get out." In time, I became so plagued by my own toxic beliefs around money, work, and success that I spent the next two-plus decades working even harder than I had on Wall Street. So much so that I woke up at age forty-nine to discover I had ended up trapped in a cult of my own making—the **Cult of Never Enough**.

To put it simply: No matter how much money I earned, accomplishments I achieved, or praise I received, it was never enough to make me feel whole inside. I was stuck on the proverbial hamster wheel, running as hard as I could but never arriving at the finish line. All this misguided energy resulted in working myself, quite literally, to the brink of death.

And my experience is not unique. Similar stories are being told right now across podcasts, magazine articles, and newspaper op-eds: People everywhere are quitting their jobs and trying to do *less*, play *more*, and embrace practices ranging from positive psychology to meditation in an attempt to experience life as human *beings*, not just human *doings*.

Yet it's still not working. Too many of us are suffering from a deeply rooted internal pressure to do more, earn more, achieve more, *be* more. And what is the result of all this achieving? Burnout, depression, loneliness, and a sense that no matter what we do, it's just Never Enough.

As a longtime member of the Cult, I've struggled with these exact same feelings. But today, I am finally free. I can look back at the decisions that drove my prior destructive behaviors with serenity and grace. And what I've come to realize is that far too many of us live our lives to optimize the soul-destroying equation of: self-worth = net worth. That's why I have written this book. I want to share a new equation, one that liberated me and will empower and set you free as well:

Financial Health + Emotional Wealth = MoneyZen

MoneyZen is a concept I coined roughly a decade ago to describe a brand of financial well-being that focuses on financial health as a precursor to emotional wealth. Back then, I'd tell anyone who'd listen that MoneyZen was a harmonious state of mind, one in which you'd finally found a sense of calm, confidence, and clarity around the role that money plays in your life.

That definition remains spot-on. But in retrospect, there was a flaw in my thinking when it came to the *actions* required to fully achieve this state. My mistake was believing that simply acquiring greater knowledge about personal finance (the "Money" part of the phrase) would naturally yield a by-product of calm and control (or "Zen"). Said differently, I thought that mastering things like successful debt management and sound investment habits would result in feelings of peace about the role money plays in our daily lives. Boy, was I wrong.

What I've ultimately come to learn is that the individual concepts of "Money" and "Zen" must be woven together to fully unleash the magic. And that's what this book will teach you how to do. Taken together, the seven chapters in *MoneyZen* give you a real-life blueprint for shedding work addiction, letting go of self-sabotaging habits, and eliminating cultish behaviors around career, money, and success—so you too can live a life of MoneyZen.

Let us launch this journey to escaping the Cult of Never Enough and reclaiming your life by first discussing what this book is *not*.

This book is not just for people who work on Wall Street, in high tech, or other ridiculously high-paying industries.

The Cult of Never Enough is open to anyone, at any income level. I've met underpaid and underappreciated teachers who are obsessed with putting in just one more hour to help a student in need, giving everything and then some to their jobs, but rarely taking time to attend to their own needs. I've had entrepreneurs show up to my office in the latest-model Range Rover and designer clothes, only to discover they are cash-strapped and awash in debt, yet unwilling to downsize their lifestyle because they have deep shame about what their friends would think if they knew just how precarious their finances were at this time. I've met full-time students with full-time jobs and massive student loan debt who feel embarrassed that they can't keep up with the spending habits of their debt-free peers, believing that their smaller bank balances somehow make them less worthy of these friendships. I've counseled frazzled moms who are the primary breadwinners *and* their families' chief caregivers, cooks, and classroom-cupcake-makers, who are scared to lighten up on all these responsibilities because somehow not "doing it all" would make them feel as if they've failed. Make no mistake, the Cult of Never Enough includes a *very* diverse group of individuals.

> This book is not a personal finance guide. It does not provide tips and advice to solve money problems.

I have already coauthored two previous books focused on **money problems** that could be solved with financial solutions. This book is very different. It addresses **money worries**—a woefully underdiscussed issue that requires emotional and intellectual solutions. We'll discuss the important distinction between money problems and money worries in greater detail in Chapter 1. For now, suffice it to say that there are many wonderful how-to books in the financial space, and this is not one of them. (You can find a robust, carefully curated list of financial resources for a variety of money problems at MoneyZen.com.)

Rather, the goal of this book is to help you understand *why* you became ensnared in your unique flavor of the Cult of Never Enough in the first place—and how to extract yourself.

As author Simon Sinek asserts in his wildly popular book *Start with Why*: "Very few people . . . can clearly articulate WHY they do WHAT they do." I believe that we get stuck in the Cult of Never Enough because we don't have a full understanding of the myriad factors that have led us there in the first place. Specifically, why do personal traumas, Counterfeit

Financial Culture, Hustle Culture, and even our own biology draw us toward a Never Enough mindset?

Unpacking these four factors, both on a conceptual level and in terms of our own lived experiences, is the focus of the first half of this book. I simply cannot emphasize this strongly enough: This knowledge is the missing ingredient required for life-transforming change.

In the second half of the book, I will introduce you to the twin concepts of financial health and emotional wealth, and show you how they can be used to create a life of MoneyZen for yourself. And because change is often easier when you know you are not alone and can learn from the experiences of others, along the way, you'll get the real-life stories of people from all walks of life who are sharing the same struggles. Woven alongside are expert insights from critically acclaimed authors, world-renowned psychologists, award-winning academic researchers, and highly regarded thought leaders in a surprisingly broad array of disciplines. They will provide you with actionable guidance that will liberate you once and for all.

In Chapter 1, we begin by examining one of the classic signs that you may be trapped in the Cult of Never Enough: You are a die-hard workaholic. Academic researchers who specialize in workaholism will provide tools for you to assess where you fall on the spectrum, explain the dangerous cognitive dissonance inherent in this obsession, and leave you with a greater understanding of the various ways in which an undue emphasis on work can play out in your life. Not sure if you're really a workaholic, or you just love your job? In this chapter you'll also learn to identify the distinctions between unhealthy work habits and healthy work engagement—and how to shift from the former to the latter.

In Chapter 2, we shift gears in a subtle but vital way. We dive into the realm of early personal experiences, the first of the four core factors that can lead to the development of a Never Enough mindset. Even seemingly small traumas, like being bullied at school or routinely ignored by a parent, can compel us to pin on our **Busy Badges** as adults, remaining constantly in motion to avoid painful feelings. You'll learn how to honor your past experiences and then transcend them, so you can tune into the emotional awareness and mental strength necessary to move forward.

In Chapter 3, we'll explore what I call **Counterfeit Financial Culture**, the societal forces that are constantly telling us we should *earn* more, so we can *buy* more, in order to *be* more. In this vicious cycle of consumption, we lose sense of what truly brings us happiness. Our lauded experts will help us understand, from a historical and sociological perspective, how these pressures came to be so dominant in our lives—and how to overcome them.

It's of no help that **Hustle Culture**, an influence we'll explore in Chapter 4, promotes and perpetuates the myth that giving everything to your job is a virtuous trait; that the meaning of life is somehow found through our career callings; or that putting in long hours will get you the executive title, the corner office, a hefty bonus. As we examine the historical underpinnings of Hustle Culture, you'll also receive step-by-step advice on how to redefine what a successful life looks like for you, personally— and how to start living it right now.

Those of us who can't seem to walk away from our desks know that overwork often feels like a clinical addiction—made all the worse by the fact that it is a socially acceptable one. In Chapter 5, we dive into the fascinating biological components that neuroscientists and addiction specialists have identified as driving forces behind our relentless *go-go-go* behavior. As our experts break down for us what's actually happening in our brains when we're in the throes of a work binge, they'll also present practical strategies for slowing it down. We'll learn how to **Unwind the Fears** that trigger our unhealthy habits, and how to **Replicate the Rewards** we receive from negative behaviors by substituting positive, healthy behaviors instead.

To recap: Chapter 1 gives you a way to assess whether you have fallen prey to the Cult of Never Enough through one of its most prevalent symptoms: workaholism. Chapters 2 through 5, taken together, provide a comprehensive road map designed to help you understand and identify the unique combination of factors that have led you to the Cult of Never

Enough—both *Why you entered* it and *Why you've stayed* in it up until this point. Armed with these specific-to-you insights, you'll now be ready to switch gears in Chapters 6 and 7 to learn *What* mindset shifts you can make to escape the Cult of Never Enough and reclaim your life.

To that end, we'll kick off Chapter 6 by breaking down the two essential core concepts that will enable you to establish a blueprint for a new life that feels true to you: **Financial Health + Emotional Wealth**. We'll dive into these two concepts from a variety of angles so that you can fully grasp how powerful they can be when serving as touchstones for your professional, financial, and personal decisions, helping you to define success on your own terms. In this solutions-focused chapter, you'll also meet a trio of experts, from surprisingly diverse fields, who will provide fascinating perspectives about how to define and nurture the twin concepts of financial health and emotional wealth in all sorts of day-to-day life decisions.

Lastly, in Chapter 7, I'll pull it all together to reveal the final secret to finding your own unique place of MoneyZen. This is where everything you've learned so far comes together, enabling you to identify your enough. This is a delightfully uplifting exercise, and the wide range of interdisciplinary experts you'll meet in Chapter 7 will provide creative and counterintuitive ideas to help you identify this all-important North Star for achieving personal and professional success. I'll also share my own time-tested **Joy-Based Spending** tools, which I've successfully used for myself, my clients, and students, to help you align your personal life vision and values with how you use your money on a day-to-day basis.

Finally, I want to encourage you to share and reflect upon any insights you've gained from reading this book. Whether in the form of a book club or a personal journaling practice, the very act of writing and talking about the factors that lead us into the Cult of Never Enough, how to escape them, and how to reclaim your life, is a powerful way to reinforce your learning and pave a stronger path toward a life of MoneyZen. At my website, MoneyZen.com, you'll find a downloadable MoneyZen Book Club Guide as well as a MoneyZen Journal, each of which offer probing questions and chapter-by-chapter reflections to consider as you read along. Alternatively, they can be handy refresher tools if you ever feel the need to revisit or reset your MoneyZen mindset as your life circumstances shift.

o o o

My own escape from the Cult of Never Enough was *very* much a two-steps-forward, one-step-back process. When I embarked upon this journey, I was highly skeptical about whether I could truly give up my addiction to work, money, accomplishments, and prestige. My behaviors felt too deeply embedded in my DNA. To my surprise and delight, over the course of absorbing and acting on the interdisciplinary research in this book, I received the most precious gift ever: I got my life back.

Today, I feel as if I have been handed a giant blank canvas, brand-new paintbrushes of all sizes and shapes, and a rainbow spectrum of open paint cans with which to play. No longer am I directed by nagging thoughts of all the tasks I should be doing, no more rushing around with my Busy Badge on. It's just me with my brushes and paint, creating the life I want to live, with all sorts of new adventures, connections, and discoveries on the horizon. My greatest hope when I broke from the Cult of Never Enough was that I'd stop feeling so bad. In my wildest dreams, I could not have imagined I'd end up feeling so good.

As you begin your own journey, be gentle with yourself and know that it is natural to struggle—and, yes, even fail at times, as you move forward. Major transformations are almost never a linear process. But thanks to the many brilliant experts and generous individuals who have shared their wisdom in this book, you can create your own custom path to freedom, reclaim your life, and experience lasting wealth. Get ready to start playing with your own set of paints, because your life is about to start bursting with color and new possibilities.

CHAPTER I

Never Enough

*"Making money your god is the fastest route
to misery and self-absorption."*

If I had to reach back in time to identify the decision that first led me to burn down my relationships, wreck my health, and wake up at age forty-nine to discover that I'd sacrificed my entire life to the altar of work—it was probably that crisp spring day in 1999 when I accepted the yellow pills from the elegantly dressed woman sitting a few rows behind me on a flight to New York. That decision sealed my initiation into the Cult of Never Enough.

At the time, I was a wide-eyed, ambitious twenty-nine-year-old, a few years out of Harvard Business School, working as an equity analyst and portfolio manager in Houston for an institutional investment management firm. Our clients were pension funds, endowments, foundations, and other institutional entities that had selected us to invest sums ranging from $10 million to well in excess of $100 million on their behalf.

The firm I worked for was managing over $50 billion in total client assets at the time. The senior executives made multiple millions of dollars a year, enjoyed second homes in upscale resort communities like Aspen and Pebble Beach, and were respected pillars of the community, serving on the boards of Houston's most prestigious nonprofit organizations.

The work was fascinating. Wearing my equity analyst hat, my job, in the simplest terms, was to analyze publicly traded companies ranging from Wal-Mart to American Express, and make recommendations as to whether we should buy, hold, or sell these stocks for our clients. Wearing my portfolio manager hat, I implemented the firm's investment strategies in my clients' portfolios, taking their needs and objectives into consideration.

Finance was, and still is, a field overwhelmingly dominated by men. But I loved the fact that the measure of success in my niche of the industry was gender-neutral: You make a recommendation and then, over time, the market tells you through the performance of the stock how accurate your recommendation was. There's no ambiguity. You're either adding value or you're not—and you are paid accordingly. A shy introvert with an eager-to-please personality (and no husband, children, hobbies, or nonwork friends to compete with my total devotion to work), I was determined to add as much value as possible.

Traditionally, the firm had served very large institutions. You had to have big bucks to get through our front door. But it was the go-go tech era of the late 1990s, and new business ideas were popping up everywhere across the country, from Silicon Valley to New York City. Back in Houston, I had a new business idea, too. I wanted to start selling a unique type of financial product that, in essence, could bring us clients who didn't necessarily have the "big bucks" minimum required for entry.

Many of the longtime senior executives weren't sold. I heard grumblings: *This will degrade our brand. It won't be profitable. Our existing clients won't like it one bit.* All valid business concerns, and they had every right to be skeptical. But their doubts only triggered an intense desire to prove myself. I wanted a seat at their table and was determined to show what I could do.

So my assistant, Jeanine, and I set about starting to build the new unit from scratch, figuring out compliance issues, operations, trading, marketing, distribution, client reporting, etc. Once the core infrastructure was set up, I embarked upon a multiyear marketing effort. Traveling up to forty weeks a year, I crisscrossed the nation, taking as many as six meetings a day to pitch our services to new clients and update existing ones. My body and brain were stuck in the "on" position: always *go-go-go*. It was not uncommon for me to get off a plane at 9 p.m., go straight to the office and work until 2 a.m., return home for a shower and brief sleep, and be back at my desk before the opening bell on the New York Stock Exchange had even rung.

That fateful day on the plane, the elegant woman must have noticed how completely depleted I was and decided to let me in on the secret. I recall that I was sitting in seat 1B, on a flight from Houston to New York. (It cost a ton more, but 1B enabled me to jump up as soon as the plane pulled into the gate and be first off, so that nothing kept me from moving forward toward more work. Overkill, I know.) My laptop was open, there were papers strewn across the tray table, tears streaming down my face. Overwhelmed and exhausted, I wasn't sure how I would make it through the dozen back-to-back meetings I had scheduled over the next two days.

But then, she approached. I can still recall her perfectly polished two-toned Chanel heels gleaming as she kneeled by my seat.

"Hello," she said, with a look that indicated an intimate familiarity with my predicament.

I'd noticed her earlier, sitting a few rows back. She was a senior executive in the industry, and I'd always marveled at her wealthy-woman hair: precision cut, frizz-free, and lustrously red. Most days, my dark brown hair was an unruly, Super Cuts special, pulled back in a ponytail because I couldn't control the way it frizzed in the Texas humidity.

She wore a sleek Armani suit, a trio of subtle yet stunning Harry Winston eternity bands, and a classic Cartier watch (one I would later procure in the same style, hoping it would magically bestow upon me equivalent poise). As far as I could tell, she never wore the same ensemble twice. Her effortless grace and style dazzled me; I was transfixed.

Staring into my eyes, she opened up a silver monogrammed pillbox and held out three yellow tablets in her perfectly manicured hand. She spoke in a hushed, almost conspiratorial tone: "Take these."

I took them eagerly, like a child grabbing at candy.

"Just a *half* of one to start," she warned. "Then later, if you need to, you can take more."

"Thank you so much," I said, wiping away tears. She solemnly nodded, then glided away before I could say more.

I swallowed half of a pill, as directed, and found that it kept my over-anxious brain calm enough to finish my work on the plane. Then I took the other half and powered through my presentations. I felt incredibly appreciative of my new benefactor.

A few weeks later, I bumped into her again at an investment conference. We exchanged professional pleasantries and she asked if the Valium had helped. It had never occurred to me to ask what she had given me. If she used them, I blindly assumed they must be okay.

"Yes, thank you," I said. "They were a lifesaver."

She nodded, opened her red Hermès bag to retrieve her pill case, and said, "Take a few more, just in case. We all use them when we need to push through."

Pushing through was all I knew at the time. I took them, gratefully.

Running her eyes up and down my outfit (sensible chunky heels and a brown knit suit—an ensemble I'd thought was the height of comfy chic), she jotted a name and phone number on a piece of paper and handed it to me.

"Next time you're in New York," she said, "you must see my stylist at Armani. Tell him I sent you."

She wasn't talking about Armani from a department store. She meant the actual flagship Giorgio Armani boutique, where the staff plied customers with champagne, and made you feel like a literal princess. Thus I learned about the world of Jimmy Choo heels and Prada handbags.

Although the elegant woman and I never became more than superficial acquaintances, I think of her as my gatekeeper into a cult of sorts. Some might call it my initiation into the cult of greed or the cult of money. But for me, it was never really about the money. It was about what the money represented: a scorecard of self-worth and a source of safety.

As I look back today, it is crystal clear that the reason I became so deeply sucked into my work was that I was desperately trying to fill a pit of shame and self-doubt that was at the core of my existence. Work was my *everything*. It was the place I turned to to hide from my pain and find protection from my fears. Receiving praise from my boss or watching a colleague's eyes widen when learning how fast the business unit was growing was my fix, my addiction. Money in the bank served as the metaphorical stockpile of anxiety-reducing, fear-blocking, pain-numbing pills on my shelf.

That fateful day on the plane, when I took the yellow pill, I embraced my new religion: the **Cult of Never Enough**. Ever dutiful, I followed the Never Enough code with gusto: *When you think you can't go on, you must find a way.* For me, that meant forgoing sleep, ignoring family, self-medicating—whatever it took to just push through and *get it done.*

Among the many rites of passage of my new cult, December heralded the start of the most important ritual: "Bonus Time." This was the moment at which you found out just how much your past year's work was worth, at least to your employer, in the form of a single number—the amount of your bonus check.

In my area of finance, base salaries were capped. But bonuses? Those had no limits. In theory, your bonus number was determined by business factors, such as how hard you worked, how much you contributed to the team, and, above all, how much money you made the company. In reality there were often other intangible elements, such as your perceived level of devotion to your work. And I was nothing if not devoted. First at my desk and last to leave? *Check.* Sweat every detail of a presentation, no matter how small? *Check.* (One tactic I'd learned from a colleague: Anytime you have to run a personal errand during work, take your wallet and car keys but leave your suit jacket on the back of your chair and your purse visibly on the floor by your credenza to make it seem as if you'd only briefly stepped away—because who would leave the building without their purse?)

It was exceptionally rare for any of us to share our bonus numbers with each other. So, part of the annual ritual was silently guessing at another colleague's bonus size based on post-holiday behaviors. For example, you might hear, come January, that a peer upgraded from a C-Class Mercedes to an S-Class, or bought an acre of raw land in Telluride, Colorado, for a future second home, and then you'd assume they *must have* gotten a better number than you did.

For some, that bonus paid for an elite country club membership, or a budding art collection, or being able to get a NetJets share and never fly commercial again. Others, like me, would sock it away every year, aiming to retire early. (But, of course, none of us would actually do *that* because that would mean you finally had enough money and there's never enough.)

Since it was taboo to talk about bonus figures at work, I couldn't wait to share my number with my parents. It makes me cringe now to think of how, every Christmas, when they would pick me up at the airport, I'd talk about money for almost the entire twenty-minute drive to their home. My mom would politely listen, albeit weary of the annual ritual. When she could take no more, she'd finally ask, "So, Mish" (her nickname for me), "how are YOU?" Without skipping a beat, I'd continue my financial monologue, adding up my base salary plus that year's interest and dividend income from my savings and investments. Then I'd flash a big smile as I announced my bonus number and shared what it added up to in terms of my total annual income and current net worth.

Sighing out of both love and frustration, my father would interject, "Munya" (his nickname for me), and share a series of Indian parables that boiled down to: "Making money your god is the fastest route to misery and self-absorption."

I'd say, "Yeah, yeah. I got it, Doof" (my nickname for him). But I was already focused on next year's bonus, because another key requirement of cult membership was to keep your number rising.

Above all, my bonus number served as a distorted external manifestation of my inner self-perception. Put another way, I had reduced my life to a single equation: *self-worth = net worth*.

Come January 1, the cycle began anew. Work harder, longer; sleep less. Self-medicate whenever you think you just can't keep going. Whatever it takes to notch another accomplishment on your resume, earn more praise, and get bigger numbers. For me, this madness was worth it to feel whole again, even if only for a short while.

By the time I'd left the Houston firm to pursue yet another set of career goals, the division I'd spent a decade building had grown to nearly $6 billion in assets under management. I loved telling people that. I still get a dopamine rush in the pleasure centers of my brain when I say it out loud—six *billion* dollars—because it sounds so darn impressive. Yet, at the same time, I also had an aching sense of disappointment—like I still hadn't accomplished enough. I felt I should have been able to grow that number even bigger. Anyone on the outside would likely have seen me as a success. But in reality, my life was in Stage 1 of unraveling.

At age thirty-nine, my marriage of just three years was already on shaky ground because I wouldn't stop working around the clock; I had lost touch with friends from college and grad school; and despite all the time and energy spent chasing professional accolades, no matter how many I received, I ached for more. I stubbornly refused to denounce the Cult of Never Enough.

I thought I was living the American Dream. It turned out to be a nightmare.

o o o

What if everything we have come to believe about "success" is actually an illusion? What if our tendency to develop our lives around the act of pursuing money and prestige has not liberated us at all, but rather has left many of us addicted to these pursuits, even as they contribute to depression, anxiety, broken relationships, and a nagging sense that what we do is never enough—that *we* are not enough?

For nearly thirty years, I was swept up in the Cult of Never Enough.

By that I mean, no matter how early I started or how late I finished work, there was never enough time. No matter how much money I made, it wasn't enough to feel like I could take my foot off the gas pedal. No matter how many accolades and awards I received, it was never enough to keep me from feeling empty afterward, like—*okay, how can I top that?* Even at the height of my lifetime financial earnings, I was constantly plagued by money worries.

I want to pause here to elaborate on the difference between **money problems** and **money worries**. There are countless financial "experts" who assert in their books, podcasts, and TV appearances that all it takes to solve your money problems is to earn more and spend less. I would argue that that's much too simplistic. Financial health doesn't come in one-size-fits-all protocols, and many money problems are exacerbated by forces beyond any individual's control.

Real-world economic issues like wage stagnation, cost-of-living increases, high inflation, affordable-housing shortages, and the fact that the top 0.1 percent of Americans hold the same amount of wealth as the bottom 85 percent—these are terrible money *problems*. The fact that teachers—the very people we entrust to help us educate and shape our children—are not paid anything remotely aligned with the value they add to society tells you something about the outlandish wealth inequality in our country. When we don't pay people what they're worth, it makes it nearly impossible for the two-thirds of Americans who are living paycheck to paycheck to earn more *or* spend less. These kinds of money problems require a wide range of financial solutions—some that are unique to your personal economic situation and some that have to do with engaging corporations, institutions, and government policy makers in fixing our larger economic inequalities.

Money worries, however, are a different beast. The money worries that we will be addressing in this book—namely, those that spring from a Never Enough mindset—beg for emotional and intellectual solutions, because they are often not about our finances at all. Instead, they are a collective aching, a feeling that *I will never measure up no matter how hard I try.*

This book is for anyone, at any income level, who feels a visceral compulsion to work more, earn more, achieve more accolades, and have more success—even at the expense of your relationships, your health, and your life. My greatest goal in writing this book is to help you shed a Never Enough mindset so you can reach your own place of MoneyZen.

MoneyZen isn't a mystical concept. It simply depicts a philosophy that allows you to make clear, thoughtful decisions around money that consistently enhance your emotional wealth. Unfortunately, most people never reach a place of MoneyZen. This book explores the reasons why—and how you can overcome them.

My workaholism was just one symptom of my Never Enough mindset. Chasing after professional success at the expense of my mental health should have been an obvious clue that I was suffering from Never Enough–itis. But I couldn't connect the dots and see that the voice in my head whispering *you are not enough* was the root cause of so many harmful behaviors.

What I call the Cult of Never Enough is similar to what Buddhists call the realm of the Hungry Ghost. Hungry Ghosts walk among us, always in search of love, understanding, and belonging. But even where there is plenty of love, understanding, and belonging, they cannot take it in because they have throats as small as the eye of a needle. They can literally never get enough.

Psychologist and author Dr. Tara Brach describes the Hungry Ghost mindset as feeling disconnected and hollow inside, leading one to chase after "substitutes" for love, understanding, and belonging. "Like drinking salt water to quench our thirst, the substitutes never satisfy the deeper need," she says. And the very awareness of our own neediness brings about even more cravings and shame. "Always wanting something different," she says, "we miss out on the life that is right here."

Just as the Hungry Ghost can never feel sated, adherents to the Cult of Never Enough never feel worthy. There's a hole in our souls that we try to fill with things like work and money, praise and success. But these substitutes can never reflect our worth as human beings.

Of course, pangs of self-doubt are a universal experience that trouble us all from time to time. This book is intended to explore how a Never Enough belief system can affect our decisions and behaviors specifically around money, work, and accomplishments. That said, I want to acknowledge that these realms are not the only playing fields in which a feeling of never being enough can wreak havoc. If you've ever felt like your friends were having intelligent conversations that you weren't smart enough to take part in, or that the Thanksgiving feast you labored to put together would never be as good as the ones your parents conjured, or that no matter how much effort and time you put into looking your best you somehow fell short—these are all the dark alleyways of a mind dwelling on the false belief that you are not enough. In researching this book, people have shared with me the countless ways in which they experience Never Enough thinking when it comes to time, money, confidence, peace, or pounds lost with their latest diet. And that's just to name a few.

When you focus on any one thing at the expense of your personal health and relationships in an attempt to feel *I am enough*, you are allowing the Hungry Ghost—no matter what form it takes—to suck the joy right out of your life.

Returning to work, it's important to keep in mind that an obsession with performance isn't necessarily driven by ego or greed. Workaholism is an equal-opportunity affliction that can affect people from any background, employed in any field, at all income levels. I've met professors who measure success by the number of citations their articles receive, graphic designers who measure their worth by the volume of projects they are working on, and podcasters on the number of downloads. Somehow, no matter what those numbers are, it's just not enough.

Here's the tricky part. Aspiring to greater career heights in and of itself is not problematic. Learning new skills and achieving new milestones can bring great satisfaction to a person's life. But when this pursuit goes too far—when your self-worth is tied up in numbers, like mine was—then you can never have enough citations, clients, or downloads. The Hungry

Ghost keeps you endlessly in search of more. As Buddhist Zen Master Thich Nhat Hanh reminds us: "Our society is designed in such a way that we produce tens of thousands of Hungry Ghosts every day."

In many ways, the cards have been stacked against us. As we'll discover in Chapters 3 and 4, modern societies perpetuate the working conditions that allow Never Enough disorders to proliferate. For example, social media is often a gateway to the types of social comparisons that lead us to believe we must do more, be more, make more money in order to measure up to our peers. Our embrace of capitalism ties us to a system that measures our very worth as human beings through our productivity levels and our spending capacity. Our employers encourage—and our peers subscribe to—a rise-and-grind lifestyle that often leads to disastrous results for our mental and physical health.

This is not just an American problem; overwork has global health consequences. In Japan, sudden death by overwork, or *karoshi*, led to 1,935 suicides in 2021. In France, executives at the country's largest telecommunications company were convicted of "institutional moral harassment" in 2019 for creating an environment of such relentless stress that it led thirty-five employees to commit suicide in a two-year period. In China, *guolaosi* is the word to describe death from overwork, and the numbers are gut-wrenching: Roughly 1,600 people in China work themselves to death *every day*.

Recently, a landmark 2021 report by researchers at the World Health Organization and the International Labour Organization found that overwork resulted in 745,000 deaths from stroke and ischemic heart disease in 2016. The majority of those deaths? They were people 60 to 79 years old who had worked for 55 hours or more per week between the ages of 45 and 74. In other words: Workaholism is a lot like smoking. Even if you quit overworking now, it can still lead to early death later.

While these may be extreme examples, they remind us that organizations (not individuals) have always been the greatest beneficiaries of workaholism—a condition in which we put work above family, friendships, our health . . . basically everything.

What does it mean to be a workaholic? The term was first coined in 1971 by psychologist and minister Wayne Oates, whose book *Confessions of a Workaholic* described it as "a person whose chronic over-involvement with work disturbs personal health and happiness and interferes with the establishment of healthy relationships." Today, the American Psychological Association's *Dictionary of Psychology* defines workaholism as "the compulsive need to work and to do so to an excessive degree." But what does that *really* look like in practice?

If you check your emails before getting out of bed, spend weekends on your laptop, and think you are too busy to take a vacation (or you spend that precious downtime on your electronic devices), you may be among the 48 percent of Americans who considered themselves "workaholics" in 2019, according to a survey by the Vision Council. Interestingly, only 28 percent of these self-diagnosed workaholics said they toiled endlessly because of financial necessity.

Psychologist Dr. Cecilie Schou Andreassen and her team at the University of Bergen, in Norway, have studied the personality traits of more than sixteen thousand Norwegian adults to create a seven-point scale that identifies work addiction. To determine where you land on the Bergen Work Addiction Scale, think about the following seven questions and jot down your answers as "Never," "Rarely," "Sometimes," "Often," or "Always."

1. You think of how you can free up more time to work.
2. You spend much more time working than initially intended.
3. You work in order to reduce feelings of guilt, anxiety, helplessness, and depression.
4. You have been told by others to cut down on work, without listening to them.
5. You become stressed if you are prohibited from working.
6. You deprioritize hobbies, leisure activities, and exercise because of your work.
7. You work so much that it has negatively influenced your health.

According to the Bergen Work Addiction Scale, if you chose "often" or "always" for at least four of the seven items, you may be a workaholic.

Researchers disagree about the exact portrait of a workaholic, but a meta-analysis of the literature by Dr. Malissa Clark and her team at the University of Georgia found the following common traits:

- Feeling compelled to work because of internal pressures.
- Having persistent thoughts about work when not working.
- Working beyond what is reasonably expected of the worker (as established by the requirements of the job or basic economic needs) despite the potential for negative consequences (for example, marital issues).

Dr. Clark, an industrial organizational psychologist and associate professor at the University of Georgia, is conducting studies that may help us better understand the causes and impacts of workaholism. She comes to this field by way of personal experience.

"Part of what drove my interest was that I struggled with it myself," she recently told me. "I've been an overachiever my whole life." By her senior year of high school, she had a 4.0+ grade point average, had held several roles on student council, volunteered as a Big Sister, played varsity soccer, ran competitive track, and served in Key Club, a community service organization. In college, she slowed down a *little*, but she still worked several jobs while being in a sorority and pulling a full load of classes.

"I think I'm still trying to figure out the core of what's driving this overachieving-type mentality," she says. "Even now, as an adult, I feel restless when I'm not *doing* something." Yet, Dr. Clark has not allowed her ambition to damage her relationships or wreck her health. So, I wanted to know: How can we tell if we're truly workaholics or if we're just *really* passionate about our jobs?

"Work engagement" is what researchers call it when one has a healthy enjoyment of their career. According to Dr. Clark, there are four dimensions to consider when trying to assess whether you are experiencing the positive state of work engagement or engaging in harmful workaholism.

1. Motivational
2. Emotional
3. Cognitive
4. Behavioral

Across all four of these dimensions, the biggest difference between workaholism and work engagement, she says, is in your underlying motivations and emotions: "With workaholism, you are being pushed to work from an inner compulsion, a feeling like 'I should be doing this. I should be doing that.' Whereas work *engagement* is when you're drawn to work, you enjoy it, and so you spend time on things because of intrinsic motivation." That's the **motivational** dimension.

The **emotional** dimension of workaholism comes into play when you're prevented from working and feelings like anxiety, guilt, anger, and irritation come up. "Like if you're at home and your kids are saying, 'Mom, look at this, Mom, look at this,' and you get irritated with them because you feel like you have to be working," she says.

The other two dimensions of workaholism include the **cognitive** component: You can't stop *thinking* about work. And the **behavioral** component: You're working all the time.

Dr. Clark warns that these two last components can look very similar in both workaholics and their nonobsessed counterparts. For example, someone who puts in long hours at the office and thinks about work when they are not on the job might not necessarily have a problem. The motivational and emotional factors that drive the behavior need to also be present for one to be considered a workaholic.

One thing I was surprised to learn from Dr. Clark is that workaholics don't necessarily achieve *more,* according to a meta-analysis of studies that looked at workaholism in the context of performance ratings. Let me repeat that: Her research suggests that when we spend endless time and energy obsessing over work, it does *not* typically result in better performance.

"There's definitely this idea that workaholics might be working for the sake of working, maybe to keep themselves busy," she says, "but it doesn't necessarily mean that they are going to be the employees who have that groundbreaking discovery or the phenomenal ad campaign." In other words, the potential benefits of putting in long hours of work—feeding the Hungry Ghost—can pale in comparison to the mental and physical costs I described earlier.

Researchers from the Beedie School of Business at Simon Fraser University and the Wharton School at the University of Pennsylvania have found that it's not so much the long hours at work that cause us harm, it's our inability to *psychologically detach* from our jobs. In a survey and health screening of 763 employees, they found that those who worked more than forty hours a week but *did not* obsess about work had fewer health issues than employees who bore the markers of workaholism. These results held even if the psychologically obsessed workaholics spent *less time* on the job than their healthier counterparts.

In a report in *Harvard Business Review*, the study authors concluded that "[w]orkaholics, whether or not they worked long hours, reported more health complaints and had increased risk for metabolic syndrome; they also reported a higher need for recovery, more sleep problems, more cynicism, more emotional exhaustion, and more depressive feelings than employees who merely worked long hours but did not have workaholic tendencies."

When I think about this, it dawns on me that I used to get probably four hours (five if I was *really* on a roll) of true, productive work completed in a day. Between Zoom meetings and responding to the endless sea of emails, the actual hours of meaningful, results-producing work for all of us is likely much less than the number of hours officially spent "at work."

For workaholics, however, it's even more insidious: We're *thinking* about work constantly. It was the first thing on my mind when I woke up and hovered there like a dark cloud as I went through my day. Even when I was doing something mundane, like pushing a cart through the grocery store or swimming laps at my local pool, thoughts about work (and self-imposed pressure to do more of it) remained. For me, the compulsion to choose work over life, industry over intimacy, has been frustratingly difficult to conquer even when I've been my own boss. At the height of my obsession, the only time that cloud lifted was when I slept. I slept a lot.

What I know for sure is that the obsessive pursuit of success, to those of us with a Never Enough mindset, has no endgame. You don't ever achieve success because you're chasing it on an unending treadmill. In fact, there's a term for it: the hedonic treadmill.

Coined by psychologists Philip Brickman and Donald Campbell, the hedonic treadmill refers to the transitory nature of our moods. No matter how happy or sad an experience makes us feel in the moment, we adapt to that new level and our moods return to a neutral state. The hedonic treadmill explains why lottery winners are not happier than nonwinners or why winning the Top Sales Associate award makes you feel amazing the first time, happy to win a second time, and the rewards diminish from there. The human brain adapts to the feeling of success so well that we need ever greater levels and varied types of accomplishments to get that rush again.

"In my field," says "Ani," a thirty-five-year-old yoga instructor from Portland, Oregon, "success is about having famous clients. Or having *lots* of people come to my classes. Or reaching mile markers, like getting the next level of yoga-teacher status or personal-training status in my certificate."

Ani enjoys her work and she's really good at it. But when she talks about her job, she admits that she feels like, whatever she does, it's not enough. "I still feel all this pressure to make more and more money, and achieve all these things," she says.

I have struggled, mightily, with the same pressure Ani speaks of. As a longtime workaholic, I was often resistant to recognizing I had a problem, let alone doing anything to change it. For example, a couple of years ago,

I took the Workaholics Anonymous "Twenty Questions" survey, which helps people like me to determine if we might have an unhealthy obsession. At the end, I tallied up my responses to queries like: Are you more drawn to your work or activity than close relationships? (*Yes*); Do you take work with you to bed? On weekends? On vacation? (*Doesn't everyone?*); Are you more comfortable talking about your work than other topics? (*Definitely.*)

Three or more yes responses indicates you may have a problem. It soon became clear to me where I was going to land on the spectrum. I answered yes to 18 out of 20 questions.

But the one question that haunted me in its specificity was this: *Have your long hours caused injury to your health?*

If working to the point of physical and mental exhaustion is a sign that you have a problem, then count me in. I've worked myself to the edge of death and vowed to slow down, twice. More about that in Chapter 5. But as you can probably guess, I was back on that treadmill faster than you could say *never enough*.

My experience may sound extreme, but it's not as uncommon as you might think. On a Sunday afternoon in April 2021, a forty-five-year-old financial consultant in London named Jonathan Frostick sat down at his home office desk to get some work done when suddenly his chest tightened and his ears popped. He was in the throes of a heart attack, and he knew it. But his first thought was: "I needed to meet with my manager tomorrow, this isn't convenient."

Hours later, while recovering in a hospital bed, Frostick began to consider the gravity of his near-death experience. He opened his LinkedIn account and made a public vow to work less. Of course, as a first-rate doer, he created a list that he posted online:

1. I'm not spending all day on Zoom anymore
2. I'm restructuring my approach to work
3. I'm really not going to be putting up with any s#%t at work ever again - life literally is too short

4. I'm losing 15kg
5. I want every day to count for something at work, else I'm changing my role
6. I want to spend more time with my family

Within hours, this workaholic's cautionary tale went viral, featured in media outlets from the *New York Times* to *People* magazine. Frostick's manifesto touched a global nerve, resonating with everyone from management consultants in Canada to entrepreneurs in Nigeria. It was the wake-up call heard round the world. To date, his LinkedIn post has collected almost 300,000 reactions and over 15,000 comments.

His dramatic story of change resonated with me, too. Because, as a thirty-year veteran of the financial services industry, I can personally attest to the fact that a near-death experience is often no match for the Cult of Never Enough. When I checked in with Frostick in the fall of 2022, about eighteen months after his heart attack, he was still finding his footing.

"Often, when you have a life event, I can imagine from the outside it's a 'Eureka' moment, you find something positive," Frostick told me. "But my Eureka-defining moment was realizing how wrong I had gotten everything. Trying to work through that lesson, whilst providing for my family, whilst sensibly trying to establish control over our finances has been a tough journey."

It's a very human tendency to think we can Do It All—that we are invincible. Some of us have to crash into the wall at 90 miles per hour, not once or twice, but three times before we accept that we must slow down.

Case in point: In a riveting 2022 episode about burnout, the *Wall Street Journal* podcast *The Journal* interviewed a thirty-six-year-old marketing professional in Atlanta named Sara McElroy, who had previously been pursuing her MBA *while* performing a full-time job, sometimes working up to twenty hours a day. But then, in June 2020, McElroy went to the ER because she was throwing up blood.

A doctor suggested she get an endoscopy, but McElroy decided she was too busy to schedule one. "It was crazy," she admitted. "I just felt like I was on the hamster wheel, and I had to keep going." A month later, she got a new job, with a more prestigious C-level title. It was a dream job on paper, but a nightmare in practice, with long hours, a hectic pace, and a toxic working environment. By January 2021 she was back at the ER, throwing up blood again. She finally got that endoscopy, and her problem turned out to be stress induced. The new job was breaking her. But she didn't reassess her priorities until she got shingles, another stress-related illness. On the last day of her doctor-ordered shingles sabbatical, McElroy turned in her resignation letter.

"The way our society works and our economy is structured, we go, go, go, and nobody really has time to pause, and stop, and think about how we fit into the broader picture and what we really want," McElroy said. Her failing health forced her to pause and ask, "Why am I putting so much effort and stock into who I am as far as my career and my identity?"

I called McElroy in October 2022 to see how she was doing. She told me that after her podcast interview went viral, she'd made yet another career move that devolved into a similarly toxic situation. So she left the corporate world to work for herself, and was writing a book to help other women determine when their job is taking more than it's giving—and it's time to quit.

"When my story first came out, the private LinkedIn messages I got from people made me realize I'm not alone," she said. Still, it took a painful process of intense introspection before she could transcend her behaviors. "I've found that more women struggle with this than perhaps we thought, because we suffer in silence," she said. "In our society, it's such a noble thing to have this great work ethic. It's idolized. So why would anyone want to admit that it's stealing our joy and hurting our relationships?"

Intrigued, I asked McElroy how she thought her past behavior had affected her relationships. "Honestly," she said, "I didn't really have any during that time. My identity was solely wrapped up in school and work. I neglected all of my personal friendships and almost completely stopped dating. I was a shell of a human and a one-trick pony. I worked. That was it."

It should be clear by now that an inability to extricate ourselves from obsessive work behaviors has deleterious effects on our physical and mental health. But the damage it does to our relationships is equally harrowing. Work addicts are often absentee parents, neglectful friends, and rotten romantic partners. In fact, divorce rates are 40 percent higher among workaholics than in couples where neither spouse overworks, according to research at the University of North Carolina.

While it would have been hard for me to recognize back then, I can see clearly now that my own marriage fell apart in part because I was *always* working, late into the night, trying to cross just one more thing off my to-do list.

At various points, I had tried course-correcting my behavior, but it never really stuck. I'd say yes to my then-husband's plans for a trip abroad, and then spend all my time on my computer in the hotel lounge. I'd say yes to a weekend of skiing with his longtime friends in Colorado, and then hole up in a spare bedroom to make work calls while they hit the slopes.

Early in our marriage, my then-husband got very interested in off-road BMW motorcycling. He asked me to join him on road trips, riding two-up, with me on the back of his bike, across South America, parts of Europe, and Asia. It was the one thing we really did together as a couple. And yet . . . while he was enjoying the scenery, I used this time to plug in my earbuds and listen to business books on Audible. While he was taking in lush landscapes and awe-inspiring mountain ranges, I was focused on "Getting Things Done" (both the book and the concept). Sometimes I'd start to fall asleep on the back of the bike from sheer mental exhaustion from all that business-think. Once, when we were riding on Germany's Autobahn at high speed, he literally had to keep reaching back and slapping my leg to wake me up because my shifting weight was threatening to tip over the bike and kill us both.

Dr. Clark's team has found that many workaholics are in denial about how devotion to work affects their families. "People who self-identify as workaholics will often say to us, 'Sometimes I wish that I would spend more time with my kids, but they know that I'm doing this because of X, Y, Z,'" she says. "But, then when you talk to the spouses, you hear a lot of the resentment, and feelings that everything is on their shoulders, and that intimacy is going away with the marriage."

What I call a self-worth = net worth mindset, psychologist Deborah Ward calls "financially contingent self-worth." Ward coined the phrase when she was a graduate student at the University of Buffalo and describes it as "a desire to achieve financial success to fulfill the superordinate goal of protecting, maintaining, and enhancing self-esteem." In a 2020 paper, Ward and her coauthors studied nearly 2,500 participants to find that people who have high levels of financially contingent self-worth suffer from loneliness, disconnection, and self-imposed pressure to work more. In a follow-up study, they turned their attention to couples and found that those of us who tie our net worth to our self-worth experience more financial conflicts with our romantic partners and less relationship satisfaction, in part because we prioritize money over our relationships. Reading that part of her study felt like a punch in the gut for me.

I'm embarrassed to admit that I've chosen to earn more money *rather* than invest in my relationships far too many times to count. There was the time I skipped my grandmother's funeral because I was too busy with some project, the content of which I can't even recall today. But I distinctly remember thinking, *Well, Gran knew I loved her. But she's dead now and I have important work to do.* It hadn't occurred to me that funerals are not about the person who passed. They're about those who are grieving and need love and support, most of all my mother.

Another time, fairly early in my marriage, my husband had a serious motorcycle accident during a weekend of off-road dirt biking in Nevada with his friends. I was in San Francisco, working in my hotel room, when he called me from his bed at the small local hospital he had been transported to in the back of a pickup truck. The doctors had told him that his injury was grave and he might lose his leg if they didn't operate quickly, so he wanted to let me know that he was heading into surgery right away. Instead of dropping everything to go be by his side, I stayed in the city two more days to finish my meetings. I cannot even remember what those meetings were about, but my logic was the same as with Gran. As my husband recovered alone in his hospital bed, I thought, *The surgery was successful. You still have your leg. You're in pain, but there's nothing I can do about it.*

As I think back on these events, I'm absolutely horrified by my behavior. But at the time, I honestly didn't see anything wrong with my decisions. The pull of Never Enough was too strong.

In some ways, I was fortunate. Many of my colleagues experienced worse outcomes. Parents whose children grew up to hate them because they were never physically or emotionally present. Bitter divorces that irrevocably ripped families apart. Vibrant individuals left broken by drug habits sparked during their pursuit of success.

Think back to a time when you chose work over human connection. Maybe you missed a friend's birthday, or a child's recital, or you stayed back at the office to secretly perfect a project, while the rest of the team went out to celebrate finishing it. In retrospect, how do you feel about that decision?

For anyone who has ever been consumed, as I was, by a Never Enough mindset, only the rarest of health or family crises could stem our *urge* to keep working. Because in our hearts, there's an indelible link between our earnings and accomplishments and the value we place on ourselves as human beings. The obsession, we tell ourselves, is worth it.

o   o   o

My bonus-chasing days are long behind me now, but I'm well aware that the Hungry Ghost will always linger just outside my door, waiting to be invited in. Any time I'm presented with the opportunity to take on a new project, I can hear the Hungry Ghost whispering in my ear, *Say yes.* And every time I finish an assignment and see the payment hit my bank account, the Hungry Ghost savors the moment and then leaves me wanting more. It has taken years to learn how to acknowledge the ghost, feel and release the pain, and then move on with *my* life.

If money and career success feed the Hungry Ghost, what makes this problem worse is that we *have* to make a living and provide for ourselves and our loved ones—we can't just quit working (or, at least, not for long).

Many of us find ourselves so severely trapped in our toxic behaviors that it meets the clinical definition of an addiction. Except that workaholism is a *socially acceptable* addiction. It's not just woven into our emotional history; it's part of the economic fabric of global capitalism. Getting *just one more task* checked off the to-do list is a social ritual that's glorified by our go-go-go culture. There are countless books, podcasts, online courses, and TED Talks designed to help us be more productive, build bigger businesses, have more followers, learn to #CrushIt. We are constantly encouraged to achieve *more*.

It's hard to resist these trends. They fuel and feed our workaholism. But even with all the clear-cut data and expertise shining a bright light on the destructive outcomes that can arise from this harmful behavior— information alone wasn't enough to make me want to step off the treadmill. Back when I was just starting to dig deep for answers and struggling to figure out *how* to slow down, I kept thinking, *Yes, I know I have a problem. I need to work less. But I can't.*

Just as Sara McElroy had to take a close look in the mirror before she could begin to reimagine her life, I too needed to do more internal work. The next step was to unpack the early experiences that had led me to the lifelong toxic belief that my self-worth was tied to a number. I needed to learn more about my *why*.

CHAPTER 2

Shame and Fortune

The power of a Busy Badge is that it can cover up all sorts of bumps, bruises, and unhealed wounds—and I suspect that many other workaholics got their badges as adolescents, just like me.

When I first met "Priya," a forty-six-year-old physician who also had an MBA degree and was starting a private medical practice, she was so deeply entrenched in the Cult of Never Enough that her long list of professional commitments was dizzying even to me.

"I live a crazy life," the married mother of two young children told me. "I consult for four companies and have five jobs at any one time. I travel every weekend and give talks internationally. . . . I've been president of state societies, regional societies. I had a baby when I was in business school and took the exam from my hospital bed."

She took a breath and, by way of explanation, said with a laugh, "I have a high capacity for work."

"Priya," I said, "what would happen if you said no to the next opportunity that arose?"

"I don't know what would happen. Because I can't say no."

"Okay," I said. "I can totally relate. But what if you replaced 'I can't say no' with 'I *won't* say no because . . .' and see what comes up for you?"

She paused for nearly ten seconds. "I mean, it's hard to unravel it all," she said. "It's all interconnected with money and status and accomplishments and success. And a feeling of safety . . . It's also the feeling of like, you know what—I'm not just a woman. I also feel I'm somewhat of a man. I think I define myself by my career and my self-worth by my net monetary value. And it's never enough."

There it was again: self-worth = net worth. And even though Priya described herself as "always overwhelmed," the very idea of doing *less* was so unfathomable to her that she wouldn't say no.

But she also revealed a fascinating insight during our conversation: Success, in essence, makes her feel like a man. This sentiment speaks volumes about how Priya's early experiences molded her. Because when I asked her to reach back and try to recall the very first time she felt like she didn't measure up, here's the story she shared:

I have this one key memory, and it's so small and yet it's so pivotal to me. I was six years old. My father was outside showing my brother how to use a camera. This was before we had digital cameras, when we still used film. I went up to my father and I asked him to show me how to use the camera, too. He said something to the effect of "You don't need to know how to use this." It was such a powerful moment in my mind. He didn't feel it was necessary to teach me how to use something that he had just explained to my brother. Like, I'm just a girl, and everybody treats me like a cute girl, or whatever. That has been a driver of so much of my behavior, my entire life. It's such a little thing but it's accounted for so many of my decisions and why I am the way I am and who I have become.

When I look at Priya, I see an incredibly talented doctor, entrepreneur, speaker, leader in her field, not to mention a loving wife and mother. She is worlds beyond that six-year-old girl who deserved to be taken seriously. Yet, like me, she has struggled with feelings that she's somehow still not enough.

I share her story because as fellow workaholics and adherents to the Cult of Never Enough, many of us hold with certainty that we *must* do more in order to measure up. This self-judgment is so pervasive, it's why Diane Fassel, author of *Working Ourselves to Death*, has called workaholism "the addiction of choice of the unworthy."

For a long time, I had viewed my work addiction solely through the lens of money. That my obsession was driven by a net worth = self-worth mindset, and the faulty belief that the more money I earned, the more valuable I was as a human being. But I can now see that money was never even the true focal point.

For instance, a few years ago, I was having one of *those* days. Operating in a state of utter chaos, I was trying to finish an essay for a women's magazine, prep for a podcast interview, finish writing a speech I was giving, review the presentation materials for a pro bono financial literacy course I was going to teach, and pack for a flight I was taking in a couple of hours. Just then a friend dropped by and caught witness to my completely overloaded calendar. She asked me: *Manisha, if someone handed you a gazillion dollars, would you still be pushing yourself so hard?*

I had to sit with that one for a while. Would all the money in the world inspire me to slow down? Not with my #CrazyBusy #HustleHarder #GetterDone mindset. These life-draining concepts had embedded themselves in my DNA. It didn't feel good. Then it dawned on me that only *one* of the tasks I was engaged in that day was earning me money.

So if my motivation wasn't solely about the money, *why* was I pushing myself so hard? Why did I say yes to all of the engagements, all the new projects and opportunities, when my schedule was already too full?

When I began digging into the research for this book, that was the very question I posed to my friend Kathleen Burns Kingsbury, a wealth psychology expert and coach, and the author of *Breaking Money Silence*. Kingsbury started her career in banking and finance, then switched to counseling individuals with eating disorders, which gave her acute insights into the mechanisms of addiction. Now, as a financial therapist and coach, she helps people work out poor behaviors around money and work.

Kingsbury's clients come to her with myriad problems: Maybe they've ignored their finances and now they're a mess, or they're afraid to talk about money with their partners, or they want to better advocate for themselves in salary negotiations. Although her specific expertise is in the area of money emotions, given her prior work with addiction I knew she would have savvy insights about the core factors driving our compulsion to hustle.

"Often, in money therapy, it isn't really about the money, it's about getting to: What is it that money represents for you? And for a lot of people, shame really cuts to the core," she said. "If we feel that there is something wrong with us, we don't feel whole, then we try to fill it. I've worked with people whose shame would present with anorexia, bulimia, and compulsive overeating. For some it can present with spending too much, or being fearful of spending at all."

As she was explaining the parameters of this idea to me, I had been silently making mental checkmarks: I have long believed that something is wrong with me (*check*); I don't feel whole (*check*); I try to fill that emptiness with work (*double check*).

But then she said something that cut me to the core, triggering a wave of fear and nausea that rippled through my body: "Manisha, your shame presents in workaholism."

At the time, I could accept that my workaholism was fueled by chronic low self-esteem, even a lack of self-worth—but *shame*? My immediate reaction to that word was to roll my eyes. It felt like such a cliché pop-psychology word (*shame, vulnerability, blah-blah-blah; what does "shame" even mean anymore?*).

Yet, on a deeper level, Kingsbury's observation that my core driver is shame made me feel *so* uncomfortable, so emotionally naked in front of her, because deep down I knew she was right.

It was a painful truth to confront. But my inability to say no tended to follow a predictable thought-feeling-reaction cycle: It started with a **thought** (*my colleague was just named CEO of a $5 billion firm*); which progressed to a **feeling of shame** (*I'll never be CEO; I am not good enough*); and then my child brain **reaction**, as Kingsbury calls it, would take over (*I need to do more*), leading me to say yes to yet another professional commitment that I did not have time for.

"One of the things that I've noticed with clients," she says, "is that the shame really seems to come from that childlike part. I picture it in my head as like you're a little girl or a little boy, and you're all by yourself, and you're in a dark room, and you're scared and you feel bad, but you don't really know how to get out of that situation."

As she was describing this scenario, sense memories transported me to my own childhood—the sound of children laughing, the buzz of the lunch bell, the smell of pine needles.

So there it is, I thought. I can't say no—I *won't* say no—because part of me was still operating in response to childhood memories and painful experiences that hobbled me with deep shame . . .

o o o

As a child growing up in Columbus, Indiana, I'd always felt like our family was special, in a good way. My blond-haired, blue-eyed mother was a vibrant college professor who hailed from upstate New York. My handsome father, the chief financial officer of a Fortune 500 company, came from a well-educated Indian family. They met in early 1969 in Rochester, New York, and married within the year. They had me in August 1970, and my brother came along seven years later. When my parents walked through downtown Columbus in the late 1970s with their mixed-race children, it wasn't exactly a scandalous sight, but it could still draw the occasional hard stare.

Staying connected to my father's family was important to my parents, so we traveled to India every other summer. After multiple connecting flights resulting in essentially a twenty-four-hour trip, we'd trudge off the plane in Ahmedabad, one of the largest cities in the state of Gujarat, in western India. After warm hugs and greetings from our extended family, who were waiting for us at baggage claim, we'd step out of the airport into the humid summer air. Before making it to the cars, we'd be swarmed by small children, drawn by the sight of my mother's blond hair. Standing barefoot with torn, dirty clothes on their thin, undernourished bodies, they begged for food and money with outreached hands. Per capita income in India was less than $300 a year then, back before the 1991 economic reforms brought more industry and commercialization to states like Gujarat.

On these trips, our days would begin with morning tea with the entire extended family, as everyone lived together in one house. Afternoon visits to my grandfather's law office or my uncle's medical clinic sent us all the way across town. On the way, I'd soak in the vibrant scene: the throngs of people moving about their day in yellow and black rickshaws, creaky buses, noisy scooters, well-used bicycles, and even the occasional ox-driven bullock cart. I'll always remember the smells, from the less-than-pleasant odor of cow dung caked along dirt roads to the delightful scent of fruits and vegetables sold at colorful open stands. One of my favorite treats was going to the lively city parks-cum-social-centers in the evening with my family to get an ice cream called Kulfi, a blend of pistachios with saffron and cardamom spices. Simply thinking about Kulfi conjures up its creamy taste in my mind.

Yet upon returning home from India, I always felt a sadness that went deeper than missing family. I'd seen so much poverty, pain, and suffering: families living in makeshift huts with no running water, electricity, or proper sanitation; elderly women and men begging at busy traffic intersections for a few coins or a bite of anything to eat; construction workers with faces of exhaustion and bodies so slight from the hard work and paltry pay for food that I feared their frames might snap in half. At home, I knew that while I indulged daily in seemingly small luxuries—hot running water and electricity on demand, a refrigerator that was always full—hundreds of millions of people in my father's homeland would never experience these privileges in their lifetimes.

When I talk about money and work with other adult children of immigrants, I often hear about the strong messaging they received growing up, sentiments along the lines of: *You'll go to college and become a doctor or lawyer. You have a duty to make us proud. You'll marry and give us many grandchildren.* In other words: We sacrificed and worked very hard to get here. And we did this so that you could fulfill the American Dream, something we didn't have the chance to do from a young age.

But I never got those messages from my parents. They didn't pressure me to get better grades or pursue wealth or marry and have ten children. For as long as I can remember, my dad has had a mantra under his Skype avatar that says, "Life's mission is to be happy." That was the loving message my parents gave me. Maybe it was seeing so much poverty in India—and being so grateful for what we had—but there was something within me at a very young age that felt an obligation to make the most of the fact that I had won the geographical lottery of being born in America.

Unfortunately, by the time I had reached fourth grade, I didn't feel like such a winner. I was no less American than any other child on the playground, yet my peers treated me as if my differences were glaring. With a strange name and mixed-race heritage, Manisha Thakor was the odd girl out. What once made me feel unique and special now felt like a burden.

What made it worse was that I was also in a physically awkward stage. At ten, I still had baby-fat rolls that made me uncomfortable in my own body. It didn't help that I was called "cow butt" and "thunder thighs" by the other kids in elementary school, or that I had braces on my teeth, thick Coke-bottle glasses on my eyes, and suffered from an itchy, scaly skin condition called psoriasis, which left thick white patches on my knees and elbows, and a daily snowfall of flakes from my scalp, making me a walking ad for Head & Shoulders shampoo.

By sixth grade, puberty hit with a new opportunity for ridicule: dark hair growing in places on my face where women weren't supposed to have hair. Back in India, parents know that bleaching, threading, or waxing are the most effective way to help their pubescent daughters get rid of unwanted facial hair. But in Columbus, Indiana, my parents were at a loss about how to help their pudgy, hairy child. One time, I snuck into my mom's bathroom drawers to find the shaver she used for her legs and ran it over my upper lip. I thought I was getting away with it, but a few weeks later, my parents sat me down on the bed and told me, "Manisha, you can't shave your lip. You're going to get razor stubble." I was mortified.

Most days, I felt so self-conscious around the other kids that I would go to the main office and check myself out of school at lunchtime. "I'm going home for my mom's Thakor taco salad," I'd tell the principal's assistant. "It's amazing!" She'd nod and smile, never knowing that my parents were both at work and my mother didn't make taco salads.

Alone with my thoughts, I'd walk the roughly four blocks to my house. While my mom was always there when I came home at 3 p.m., she taught during the day and our doors were locked at lunchtime. I was too ashamed to explain to her what was going on at school and ask for a house key. Instead I'd sit under the picnic table in our backyard or under the big pine tree at our neighbors' house, both of whom were also teachers and at work. These were my hiding places, literally and figuratively, until the emotional dangers of school cafeteria time were over.

I practiced this lunch hour ritual with such regularity that on parent-teacher night, the principal's assistant came up to my mom and said, "I hear you make the best taco salad!" I thought I was busted, but my mom just smiled. Later I heard her tell my dad, "Wasn't that an odd thing to say?"

At some point I accepted that it was useless trying to make friends. The boys ignored me. The girls were cruelly dismissive. But my *teachers*. They were excited to have a student who was genuinely interested in what they were saying. They saw my eyes light up with curiosity. They encouraged me to shine.

The respect of my teachers became my new refuge. I vowed to be the most interested, sharpest listener, hardest studier, top-of-the-class kind of kid. All the social advantages I had been deprived of in my formative years—a best friend to share secrets with, post-football-game bonfires, playing Spin the Bottle, and rowdy, summer pool parties—I traded all of it for the validation of my instructors. Never again was I going to be remembered as thunder thighs. I would be known as the high school valedictorian, voted Most Likely to Succeed, a Phi Beta Kappa graduate from Wellesley College who spent a year studying abroad at Oxford University and earned her MBA from Harvard Business School.

When I entered the working world, my metrics changed. Instead of pleasing my professors, I sought the approval of my bosses. Instead of straight A's, I earned ever-higher bonus numbers. All of it was fueled by a flickering shame from feeling less-than, unwanted, not good enough—a shame that burned deep beneath the surface, where I didn't have to face it.

Instead of confronting my emotions, I pledged my life to the equation of self-worth = net worth. I told myself that my obsession with career achievements represented my response to a society that asks within thirty seconds of meeting you, *What do you do?* and then judges you on your answer. I was certain that my drive to earn ever-higher bonus numbers simply represented my strong desire for financial independence. After all, as my mother once told me, *money gives women voices and choices.* Of course I wanted that. Also, like so many women I meet, I harbored a secret, visceral fear of ending up the proverbial bag lady, living old and alone under a bridge somewhere. In other words, I thought that my behavior was a rational reaction to external realities.

External factors do push us to overwork, and we'll explore those influences in Chapters 3 and 4. In my case, the surface-level reasons I gave myself for why I was a workaholic—they were all true. But if I'm being *really* honest, my addiction to work during those years was also driven by grade school traumas that took up residence in the crevices of my sense of self. Deep down, I had believed that if I just had enough money in the bank and accomplishments under my belt, I would never again be stuck in a situation where I felt dismissed and diminished by peers as I did growing up.

Having struggled with mental health over the years, I've seen my share of therapists. During my twenties and early thirties, simply talking about those schoolyard experiences would have caused me to tear up. Today I view my past with grace. I feel compassion for who I was back then, and pride for who I have become today. The painful memories are no longer emotionally triggering to talk about. But when Kingsbury first introduced me to my own hidden feelings of shame, it was hard for me to stomach the idea that something as seemingly benign as being teased or feeling terribly unpopular as a youth could be a gateway to a lifelong obsession with work and money.

Yet a significant body of scientific research clearly indicates that childhood traumas can manifest in adulthood as depression, substance abuse, and a variety of harmful coping mechanisms, including workaholism. A 2013 study on survivors of childhood sexual abuse found that some victims overworked as adults as a way to escape their memories. As one subject stated, *I became a workaholic . . . to avoid even thinking about the issues or anything else, I threw myself into work night and day.*

Clearly, my schoolyard experiences pale in comparison to the severe or life-threatening traumas experienced by others. But like many workaholics, my history aligns with something called little-*t* or small-*t* traumas, which refer to distressing events that make us feel so helpless that we are unable to emotionally cope. Research funded by the National Institutes of Health indicates that being bullied as a child "can affect physical and emotional health, both in the short term and later in life . . . and can cause long-term damage to self-esteem."

However, there is very little research on whether feelings of isolation as a child can lead to workaholism as an adult. I turned to one of the world's foremost workaholism experts to ask, *Could all those years of schoolyard stress really be the cause of my chaotic calendar?*

"Oh, absolutely," says psychotherapist and *Chained to the Desk in a Hybrid World* author Dr. Bryan E. Robinson, who studies workaholism through the lens of child and adult development and has been helping clients tackle work addiction for more than twenty-five years. "When you're in that stage of identity-role confusion, to feel like a failure or to feel bullied, we introject those experiences and they determine how we feel about ourselves. Then, so we can live our lives fully, we have to find a way to fill that hole, and often it's by producing or exceling at something."

"I'm working with someone right now who is convinced that they have to work longer and harder than the average person just to keep their job," Dr. Robinson told me. "But that's a perceptual distortion. Just like someone who has anorexia will look in the mirror and see themselves as overweight when they're only ninety pounds, workaholics also have these perceptual distortions that feel real. This is developmental. This doesn't just come out of the air. This comes from trauma and certain childhood experiences."

Dr. Robinson says that the origin stories of many workaholics "share an emotional blueprint: isolation, pain, loss, fear, and sometimes embarrassment. We are comrades of the soul bound together by common childhood wounds."

He would know. As a self-described "workaholic poster child," Dr. Robinson grew up in an unstable home with an alcoholic father, who was violent and unpredictable, and often abandoned him and his younger sister. In his book, he tells how he became "the protector, the peacemaker, the referee, the judge, and the general" of his family—at just nine years old.

In hundreds of interviews with workaholics that Dr. Robinson has conducted both in his private practice and in research at the University of North Carolina at Charlotte, he's found that many work addicts experience "parentification" as children—meaning, they were thrust into adult responsibilities before they were psychologically ready. "What that looks like, and these are real examples," he tells me, "is that you're paying the light bill, the gas bill, you're taking care of your younger siblings and you're twelve years old."

Dr. Robinson's response to parentification was to lose himself in schoolwork, housework, church activities, and, later, the working world, toiling nights, weekends, and holidays—even hiding his work, just as his father had hidden his bottles of booze.

"As an adult," he writes in *Chained to the Desk*, "I came to realize that I had cultivated the use of work to conceal emotion and my true self instead of expressing them. Believing my family problems were unique and shameful, I strove to gain control and approval by excelling in school and the world outside my home."

There's that word again: *shame*.

Just like Kingsbury, Dr. Robinson believes that shame is often at the core of workaholism, or any addiction for that matter, and that my obsession with being busy may be an attempt to override the discomfort of shame.

"Sometimes we are aware of our feelings of self-inadequacy because we have an inner critic that reminds us a lot that we're not okay or that we're not as good as other people or we can't perform as well as other people," he says. "But most people don't always know they have shame or that they feel ashamed, because shame is carried deeper in the dungeons."

It was hard at first to accept that feelings of shame lurked deep in my dungeons, or that I derived a sense of worth from an overpacked schedule. But I can see now how the chaotic calendar I hewed to made me feel important.

Being someone who was *always* on the go meant: *I'm needed; I'm successful; people want me.* I used to wear chaos like it was an honor: *Look at me! I've got my Busy Badge on.* At the same time, it also represented a new picnic table to hide under: *Sorry I can't go to your dinner party, girls' night out, group vacation . . . because I have too much work.* Not even attempting to connect meant I never ran the risk of not "fitting in" with the gang, not being rejected.

Adolescent traumas, even the small-*t* kind, as Dr. Robinson notes, can leave a hole in your psyche that grades, awards, accomplishments, and money cannot fill no matter how much we try. The power of a **Busy**

Badge is that it can cover up all sorts of bumps, bruises, and unhealed wounds—and I suspect that many other workaholics got their badges as adolescents, just like me.

Last year, I sent a totally nonscientific survey to my MoneyZen newsletter subscribers—friends who know me from my books, media appearances, and consulting work. Kind of like a Rorschach test, the survey asked them to free-associate and write down the very first feelings and impressions that came to mind when they thought of the phrase "Never Enough." In just twenty-four hours, I had more than one hundred responses, many of them heartbreaking. Here are a small handful:

- Lacking in some way no matter what I do.
- I think of my mom and the story that she tells herself about herself; I think of the young girl inside of me that doesn't always think she belongs and is different from everyone else.
- Work more and longer to be enough.
- My life. What I heard from my father.
- There is always something else I can do, perfection doesn't exist, the game never finishes.
- Not good enough, endless striving.
- "Can't you do anything right?"–famous quote from my mother to me!

Honestly, I had been expecting sentiments more along the lines of *I'm not sure if I have enough money invested for retirement*. And I did receive several responses from individuals who felt insecure about their financial health. But the majority of respondents came to me with answers that pointed to feelings of emotional poverty.

In a follow-up survey, I asked these same friends to think about a time when they were volunteering or working to a degree that was unreasonable and having a negative impact on their lives. Presented with a long list of factors that may have played a role in their urge to be busy, they could check any factor that applied. The top three reasons: "Expectations I set on myself" (75 percent), followed by "Experiences in adolescence that make me feel like I have to do more to prove myself" (44 percent), and "Propensity of my workplace to reward overworking" (34 percent, and an important topic that we will cover in Chapter 4).

Like the Hungry Ghosts we talked about in Chapter 1, there are millions of us out there trying to fill the void with more work, more opportunities to prove that we are enough. As wealth psychology expert Kingsbury notes, some of her most professionally successful clients frequently and consistently tell her: "I'm not doing enough."

"I also hear a lot of perfectionism, a lot of black-and-white thinking— *I'm not doing it right. I'm doing it wrong*—that usually gets down, at a deeper level, to shame, to family stuff that they were raised with and experiences that they had," Kingsbury says.

That was certainly the case for "Lauren," a forty-eight-year old finance executive from California, who says that her compulsion to strive beyond reason stems in part from cultural conditioning, part gender bias, and part self-imposed perfectionism.

"In my Korean culture, we are conditioned at a very young age to push ourselves, have high expectations, work hard. And unfortunately there is a lot of bias toward gender," she said. "So women who work are *also* supposed to be one hundred percent good moms, good wives, and good daughters. Subconsciously, I put the pressure on myself more than others pressure me."

Born in Seoul to a stay-at-home mom and an educator father, Lauren and her family moved to the States when she was a toddler, then back to South Korea when she was in third grade. Finding herself in a new school, where she didn't understand the language or the customs, Lauren felt like an outsider in her own country. She easily recalled the small-*t* traumas she experienced at this early age: "I got bullied from my classmates. People were like, 'Oh, look at that girl. She doesn't even speak our language. What is she wearing? What's her haircut all about?'"

When Lauren had trouble at first with her homework assignments because of the language barrier, even her third-grade teacher antagonized her. "It was 'Oh, you didn't do your homework? Come over here, you get fifty push-ups,'" Lauren recalled. "It was disheartening to understand that the only way I was going to get respect was by being excellent. That's what drove me: I needed to be flawless. That's where the perfectionism comes in."

An obsession with perfection pervaded Priya's childhood as well. Growing up in a strict Indian household, Priya told me, she "was not allowed to make mistakes. In the morning, my brother and I dressed ourselves. We sat quietly. We'd always clean all the plates. I remember going to the American family's houses for car pool. The other kids, they're still in their pajamas, they're running late, they're watching TV, cereal's hanging out of their mouth. But we're on the sofa in our uniforms with our backpacks on, our hair is done, and we're sitting carefully."

Lauren, who self-identifies as a people-pleaser, had similar experiences.

"I so deeply wanted my mother to just see the positive things about me," she said. "Even to this day, I'm forty-eight, she comes over, we didn't see each other for two and a half years because of Covid, the first thing she says is 'Lauren, you've got to do something about your face. You've aged so much. All the women your age in Korea have flawless skin.' I didn't know what to say to her!" Lauren laughed good-naturedly as she recalled their awkward reunion. She can talk about it now with a sense of humor because over the years, she says, she's learned "how to let it go, and how to accept myself."

Priya's and Lauren's experiences speak to one of the most common problems I see among women who strive to do it all: extreme perfectionism. Extreme perfectionism, which appears to be steadily rising across all generations of young adults, can lead to terrible mental health consequences, including anxiety, depression, eating disorders, and thoughts of suicide, according to a longitudinal study of American, Canadian, and British college students from 1989 to 2016.

Of course, perfection is an impossible benchmark. Humans fail constantly, and we learn and grow from our mistakes. But if our entire identity is tied up in a desperate drive to always be perfect, then when we fail we're left with debilitating feelings of shame and low self-esteem.

To be fair, Lauren's and Priya's parents loved their daughters very much and did the best they could to raise them according to their core values. To all appearances, both women's lives turned out quite well. Priya has proven that she is more than capable of success in multiple realms, not just the ones deemed suitable for her gender. Lauren grew up to become a successful professional, and a good mom, wife, and daughter, as her parents expected. But deep down, both women have struggled over the years with oppressive thoughts that they needed to do more, *perfectly*, in order to measure up.

"It's hard sometimes," Priya says. "Am I doing things right? Maybe nobody knows. You just want some really smart person to pat you on the head or tell you, 'This is what you need to do now.'"

This high level of internal pressure is a hallmark of workaholics. Recently I spoke to "Dominique," a thirty-six-year-old teacher from Los Angeles and a self-described "consummate overachiever and people-pleaser." Dominique told me that she suffers from anxiety, exhaustion, and health problems because she won't say no to additional commitments. Whether it's more responsibilities at work, or volunteering for her children's school and sports activities, Dominique struggles with the feeling that she should be raising her hand every time.

"I manage to find a way to do all of the things for all of the people and I very rarely ever have time for myself," Dominique said. "Honestly, sometimes I'm like, 'Can I ever just be the parent who drops off my kid and watches the game? Do I have to be the one to do the snack schedule, and print the scorecards, and organize the banquet? *Really?*' But I just can't quiet the voice that says, 'Do more.'"

Dominique has always done more. As a young woman, she was accepted into one of the top magnet high schools in California, based on her grades and test scores. Surrounded by overachievers, she was one of just six Black students in her graduating class, and she felt immense internal pressure to prove that she belonged. In college she entered the honors program with a double major and finished magna cum laude in four years. She was a resident assistant, pledged with a sorority, served as vice president and then president of the African Student Union, served on the school's judiciary board, and worked at an internship with a major television network.

Later in life, when Dominique found herself mired in a toxic work environment, her initial response was to work *harder*, prove you can take it. Her body revolted and she had to deal with serious health issues, including a miscarriage and a cancer scare, which she's still processing.

"It taught me to be more aware of what's going on, to listen to my body, and to not allow myself to get to the point where my body is attacking itself to get me to stop working," she said. "But it's still really a hard struggle for me."

Dominique is intelligent and self-aware. She knows that her Never Enough lifestyle is unsustainable. But the neural patterns run deep. It's hard to quiet the voices that have been directing us since childhood.

When I ask Dominique to reach back to her earliest feelings of not being enough, she tells me she grew up with a successful schoolteacher mom, who was supportive and loving, but that her father was not involved in her life. Dominique decided at a young age that she and her mother were fine without him.

"In my mind, I was like, well, if he doesn't want to be around, then I'm going to prove that I don't need him. I'm not going to be a statistic. I'm not going to ever allow somebody to say, 'Oh, well, it's because she's from a single-parent household,'" Dominique said. "That's still so much of a drive for me, which is hard to admit."

In fact, Dominique's father had passed away a few weeks before our first conversation, and she was still wrestling with how his absence in her life had impacted her emotionally.

"All of these feelings of self-worth and self-esteem and abandonment and there not being any resolve or reconciliation, all of that is still . . ." She paused to collect her thoughts. "The fact is that so much of what I do and how I behave or decisions that I make are based off of that. And that's something difficult that I'm having to come to terms with now, too."

o o o

Priya, Lauren, Dominique, and I all experienced fairly common emotional wounds as adolescents that left us with deep feelings of shame. Our small-*t* traumas didn't break us, though. We pinned on our Busy Badges, piled on the projects, and got about the business of proving our worth. As children and even into adulthood, it was a survival mechanism. For me, I got about the business of making as much money as I possibly could, so that the cheerleaders could never again spread their lunch trays out on the table when I was coming over so that there was no space for me to sit down.

But what if, as an adult, we don't need to wear our Busy Badges anymore? What if they have far outlasted their original usefulness? How do we find the confidence to take them off? And how do we break the habit of the reflexive "yes" to any new project or opportunity?

Kingsbury encourages her clients to parent the child part of our brain that's desperate to take over and react impulsively. In effect, she's telling Priya to be that really smart person who pats herself on the head and says, "It's okay, you're doing enough." She's inviting Lauren to be the adoring mother who appreciates how beautiful she already is, just as she is. And she's encouraging Dominique to be the loving parent who practices self-care and kindness to that overachieving child who has already proven she is a superstar.

Additionally, Kingsbury advocates for slowing down our decision-making process. In those moments when we are struggling to decide whether to take on new commitments, it helps, she says, to pause first. "Tap into your adult brain, take a step back, and ask yourself: Does this make sense for me? What is going to make me the happiest and healthiest in this situation?"

If you're still unsure, or if deciding *right now* feels too hard, then lean into "the power of maybe."

"We're in a society where you're expected to decide quick, you've got to keep going, going, going," she says. "But with the power of maybe, your response is 'You know what? Maybe. But I need to slow it down.' And then get in touch with what you're feeling and what you need, so you can make the right decisions for you."

Thinking with your adult brain is showing compassion to your child brain. You're giving her a break. You're allowing yourself to breathe and explore what will bring you joy.

And when feelings of shame and Never Enough creep back in?

"If you've lived your life being driven by 'Never Enough,' then it *is* awfully scary to think, 'Oh God—is *this* enough?'" Kingsbury acknowledges. "So you have to start with 'Okay, that small child inside me, who probably feels a lot of shame—what does she need to do to take care of herself?'"

Dr. Robinson also suggests such practical steps as "work moderation plans" that allow for self-care, playtime, and relationship nurturing in your schedule; putting boundaries around your work hours (for example, no work beyond 8 a.m. to 5 p.m.); and setting cushions of fifteen minutes or more between appointments to give yourself time to stretch and renew. In his practice, he helps clients to calm the stressful fight-or-flight physiological response that obsessive thoughts induce in our brains. The antidote to those high-stress ruminations, he told me during our call, is to activate our parasympathetic nervous system, the network of nerves that slow our heart rate and breathing and help us to feel calm.

"That means relaxing with a bubble bath, getting a massage, meditating, taking a walk, or just breathing," he said. "Unfortunately, workaholics will often say they don't have time for these things. They don't realize that it will make them more productive and feel better about themselves in the long run. Instead, they're rushing to get as much done as they can, multitasking, which we know does not serve us at all."

I am mortified to admit that as he was telling me this very good advice, I was quite literally checking work emails on my computer. In other words, I was multitasking and thinking to myself, *A bubble bath—who has time for that?*

If detaching from work was this hard for me—someone who is self-employed, with enormous flexibility in her schedule, a comfortable financial life—I feel incredible empathy and frustration for my comrades of the soul who are fighting this addiction while also struggling to pay their bills, care for family members, or overcome the myriad financial challenges so many people face today. Most people *have* to work. We can't just abstain from making a living. So what is a workaholic to do?

A lot of the work, Kingsbury says, comes with tolerating the feelings of discomfort, and showing yourself compassion. Take small steps at first if it helps. For example, start by spending an hour a day, at any time that works for you, just thinking to yourself, *I am enough.* When self-denigrating thoughts arise? Cut them off at the pass with "I am enough."

"Clients laugh at me when I tell them this," Kingsbury says. "But I'll say, 'No, really. Try it. If you can tolerate thinking *I am enough* for an hour, great. If you can't, five minutes is good. And then you can go back to *never enough.*'"

How do you feel when you close your eyes and think about the phrase *I am enough*? Pause for a moment and let your mind go there. What bubbles up for you?

If you're stubbornly clutching your Busy Badge like I was back when I first tried this exercise, it may not go so well. That's okay. A feeling of resistance, even deep skepticism, is part of the process. I recall thinking, *I am enough. I am enough. I . . . have so much on my to-do list I should be getting to, WHAT A STUPID EXERCISE!*

But today I'm reminded of a Carl Jung saying, which boils down to: *What you resist persists.* That's where I live in this moment: in less denial about my feelings of shame, slowing down some; my Busy Badge in a drawer, for now. There was a time when I couldn't talk about my childhood experiences without crying. But now I can clearly connect the dots to how they contributed to my Never Enough mentality and I look back at those years with compassion for that little girl, not shame or grief.

If I've learned anything from this journey back to childhood, it's that shame and little-*t* traumas are a surprisingly powerful piece of the puzzle for many of us. Yes, we can transcend these events. We can parent the scared inner child. We can shed the false narratives that convinced us we were not enough. Yet often our awareness of these internal narratives is still not enough to stop a toxic relationship with money, work, and success.

The road map to healing requires more from us than just saying "No." Personally, as much as I would have loved to step away from my computer and take a bubble bath after talking with Dr. Robinson, I found it really difficult to change my behavior at first, because we live in a society that continually encourages and praises our urges to be, do, and have *more*.

As I would soon learn, I had yet another step to take: armoring up to fight the external narratives—the powerful societal practices and signals that lead us to believe we can never measure up to our peers and their accomplishments.

CHAPTER 3

Striving Ourselves Crazy

"It's like almost the gamification of life. You have to get these numbers; your life has become like a video game."

A travel journalist friend once told me that when he arrives at a hotel for a press trip, the other writers in attendance typically get there around the same time. One day, as he was waiting to check into his room, he noticed another journalist checking out his luggage. That's when he realized that all the other writers in line with him had beautiful, silver hardcase bags and various high-end brands of well-made luggage. Suddenly he felt incredibly self-conscious about his large, red-fabric suitcase with bulky wheels and fraying seams—a dowdy but dependable department store purchase.

My friend immediately bought new luggage when he got home. Nothing expensive, just a sleek black hardcase that would visually express that he too lived a worldly, on-the-go lifestyle. Like a bird that signals his prowess through his feathers, he wanted this suitcase to signal both how he saw himself and how he wanted the other journalists to see him.

His story reminded me of the purses I owned when I worked in high-net-worth finance. My "four-digit" handbags—what I called any purse that dared to cost over $1,000—were how I signaled my worth to my flock.

At twenty-eight, I purchased my first four-digit purse, a classic Chanel shoulder bag, made of buttery, black-quilted leather, with a single fold-over flap and a gold chain-link strap that was shockingly heavy. Walking into a meeting room to visit a prospective new client, I'd stride in with my Chanel bag prominently dangling off one arm while carrying my presentation materials in the other.

Of course, you had to be on your A-game in these meetings to be taken seriously, and as a devoted workaholic, I was always very well prepared. But my purse gave me an extra bit of sparkle. Just as my friend noticed that the hotel valet was a little more deferential after he started carrying better luggage, I noticed the people in the meeting room sitting up a little straighter in their chairs when I put that iconic four-digit bag down on the conference table. If the receptionist saw me walk in with it, there would be a subtle shift in the way they placed a cup of coffee on the table for me, compared to the days when I used to walk in with my perfectly good, albeit very well-worn department store carry-all.

What's ironic about my penchant for status bags during that period of my life is that lavish spending, in general, made me so uncomfortable. My style was to hover around the edges, out of the limelight. When my contemporaries working in finance, law, and management consulting were buying starter homes in the fancy neighborhoods of Houston, I moved into a loft complex that was on the other side of the tracks from those neighborhoods, both literally and figuratively from a status standpoint. When everyone began collecting upscale art to hang on their walls, I found interesting black-and-white pictures online and would pay the photographers for the rights to reprint them in a larger size and place them in nice frames, resulting in striking pieces that cost one-tenth of my colleagues' purchases. While my peers planned meticulously lavish weddings in their late twenties, and began interviewing nannies shortly thereafter, by contrast, at age thirty-five, I wore a lovely satin dress from J.Crew and had a mere eight people present when I married a man twenty years my senior, who didn't want more children and didn't mind, at least at first, that I worked *all the time.*

So that's why it's embarrassing to admit that the supersparkle power I got from my pricey handbags was a total rush. At home, I'd wear blue jeans and T-shirts. But at work, I donned my battle gear: power suits, high-end heels, and luxury purses. And while my travel journalist friend stopped after buying one suitcase, I bought more and more battle gear to fortify my defenses. In my closet was a battalion of leather and gold soldiers: the Lady Dior bag created for Princess Diana, the classic Ferragamo top handle, a Gucci clutch, a Prada large enough to carry my laptop and work papers, and of course, more Chanel handbags of every shape, size, and style. I peaked at about twelve status purses.

But then something interesting happened when I left the corporate world. I was thirty-nine and heading into an entrepreneurial chapter of my career. My then-husband and I decided to move from Houston to a sun-drenched, minimalist desert home in Santa Fe, New Mexico. The master bedroom in our new house had double closets, so one of the very first things I did in mine was to hammer hooks into the wall to hang all my purses on, like an armory, so I could select the bags I would carry with me into that day's battlegrounds.

Except, I wasn't actually doing battle anymore. In my new life I was writing books, teaching personal finance workshops, and making media appearances. Having a pricey handbag on my arm as I walked onstage to give a keynote speech was not going to wow the audience. They wanted financial advice for the real world—not a reminder of how much money I could afford to waste on a purse.

And the people I met in Santa Fe? They did *not* carry the purses that executive women in finance from New York to Los Angeles did. It would have looked ridiculous for me to walk into town with my Manolo Blahnik heels and Balenciaga handbag, surrounded by a sea of cowboy boots, turquoise jewelry, and boleros. No, my battle gear stayed on that closet wall, gathering dust.

With each passing year, it became clear to me what a wasted investment opportunity they represented. Occasionally, I would look at that closet wall, the financial gears turning in my mind, and think to myself: *There is nearly twenty thousand dollars' worth of handbags gathering dust in here. If I'd invested that amount of money in the S&P 500 instead of all this stupid leather hanging on my closet wall, how much would I have made by now?* I started calling it my "Wall of Shame."

Eventually I gave away the majority of my suits and heels to Dress for Success, an organization that provides low-income women with business attire to help them land jobs. While I kept a few purses to use when visiting corporate offices for periodic consulting work, I gave the rest away to girlfriends for whom that buttery soft leather armor would still be professionally useful.

I'd like to tell you those handbags no longer have sparkly power for me. But the truth is, I still get a tiny *zing* when I carry one, because I see others' reactions and, for a moment, I feel special. The difference is that I *know* that feeling will be fleeting. The sparkle doesn't last. I see these purses for exactly what they are: external objects that I once used to measure internal value. Imbuing status items with this kind of meaning is a mistake many of us make, every day.

o   o   o

From a very early age, we are bombarded by deceptive messaging that draws our attention toward what we have and what we do. As we move through our social and professional circles, comparing our lot to our neighbors', we begin to believe that what we have is not enough, what we earn is not enough, and therefore we are not enough.

But this messaging is an illusion; it's based on a set of beliefs and trends that I refer to as **Counterfeit Financial Culture**. We place added value on expensive objects and experiences—be they haute handbags, status watches, or pricey memberships at trendy gyms where we work out in the latest must-have $150 yoga pants. These are all bogus barometers of our value as human beings. Intellectually, we know this. But the societal forces that lead us to believe we need to do more and have more in order to be deserving of respect—of a chance at the American Dream—they can be simultaneously powerful and subtle.

For a workaholic, when the *external* forces of Counterfeit Financial Culture meet the *internal* forces of the Hungry Ghost, it's enough to send their Never Enough mindset into overdrive. We feel an unrelenting pressure to keep up, not just with our neighbors and colleagues, but with the expectations we place on ourselves.

When it comes to Counterfeit Financial Culture, I've observed two powerful forces that I believe are "striving" us crazy: 1) Flawed Self-worth Anchors, and 2) False Financial Comparisons.

Let's unpack these a little more.

FLAWED SELF-WORTH ANCHORS

Flawed Self-worth Anchors are any external possessions, symbols, accomplishments, numbers, titles, experiences, or credentials that give us a false sense of worth or make us believe that others must be more happy, successful, and fulfilled because they possess this anchor. When we buy into Flawed Self-worth Anchors, we are perpetuating the myth that our identity and our value is directly tied to what we do for a living, or how we spend our money, or the titles and credentials we use to signal our place in society.

"All those sparkly and shiny and seductive things—we've been told by advertising since the 1900s that we *need* all those things," says psychotherapist and *Emotional Currency* author Dr. Kate Levinson. "Our culture is constantly sending messages about what it values, and those messages for over a hundred years have said: 'More is better.'"

Collecting more four-digit purses sure seemed better to me when I worked in an elite investment firm in Houston. But when my personal and professional realms changed, those purses weren't brilliant tail feathers or armor anymore. They revealed my otherness. As a new resident of Santa Fe, New Mexico, a town that prides itself on local traditions and a laid-back vibe, my purses signaled that I was clearly not part of this community and certainly not a member of the business elite. They preferred the four-digit cowboy boots and pricey shearling coats that signaled to those in the know that even though the local culture was salt-of-the-earth, their salt was very expensive. And that's the problem with Flawed Self-worth Anchors. Their perceived power is slippery and deceptive due to the fleeting nature of what's hot and what's not in your current comparison group.

As we go through life collecting flawed anchors, we tend to size up the relative individual value an anchor lends to our sense of self. For example, the travel journalist who felt like his dependable old suitcase failed to reflect his professional standing was placing a *small* measure of his self-worth in a piece of luggage. So is the teenager who spends his entire summer earnings on a pair of trendy sneakers because he thinks they'll make him look cool on the first day of school.

On a one-off basis, these anchors can be harmless. But without a clear perspective about the values and character traits that *actually* signify a meaningful life, the pursuit of Flawed Self-worth Anchors can actually lead us toward crushing errors in judgment. Like when the parents involved in the 2019 college admissions scandal paid bribes, falsified test scores, and conjured fake sports accomplishments for their children because they perceived that certain "elite" schools were such valuable anchors—for their children and for themselves—that they would lie, cheat, and steal someone else's opportunity in order to secure their own child a place.

As Dr. Levinson told me, it can be hard to unhook ourselves from Flawed Self-worth Anchors that are entrenched in the values of our society. "Our country was founded on the idea that more is better: *More land? Take whatever you can, you're a fool if you don't take it, and it doesn't matter who you're hurting or who you're stealing from. We're supposed to have more,*" she said. "More moves the wheels of commerce. But what would it be like if we could use that same energy to feed more people instead of consuming more? It's a revolutionary question to ask: *What is really important here? Is this really benefiting me? Is this benefiting the world?"*

In a culture that perpetuates the illusion of Flawed Self-worth Anchors, it's important to occasionally reassess the anchors in our own lives. For example, it may be helpful to ask: *Does this extra cost make sense for us, financially?* Yes, you need to shelter your family, but maybe you don't need a house with a pool. Maybe the kids don't need their own bedrooms. Or, if these things are important to you, are you able to accept the trade-offs, like less money left over for retirement or college savings? You can also ask: *Does this object or experience support my authentic self?* In other words, do you really want and need the latest-model smartphone? Weren't you just saying that you'd like to spend less time on your devices?

Sometimes, when we're uncertain of an anchor's true value, we can see it more clearly by measuring the missed opportunities they may represent. For example, it's not lost on me that my Wall of Shame purses could have fed a family of four in the U.S. for an entire year; or purchased 150 more suits for the Dress for Success mentees; or paid for the annual school supplies of two hundred students in need. In recent years I've begun to focus more on contributing my time and charitable giving to causes supporting women's economic empowerment and well-being. Those darn purses used to weigh me down and leave me hungry for the next year's model. By contrast, my new community-based pursuits leave me feeling lighter, better connected to people and ideas outside myself, and liberated from the constant need for more.

Work is a classic realm in which humans collectively buy into each other's Flawed Self-worth Anchors. Here's an example that almost everyone can relate to: Think about the last time you were introduced to someone at a party. Did the host announce that person's occupation by way of introduction? Maybe she said, *I want you to meet Marc, he's a surgeon at Children's Hospital.* Suddenly Marc is more interesting, smart, and sexy than when he was just a guy with a mustard stain on his tie.

But what if our occupations did not dictate our perceived worth?

What if the host said, *This is Marc, he has seven siblings, twelve nieces and nephews, and a brand-new puppy.* Or *This is Marcy, she loves to collect vintage stamps and read biographies in her hammock.* In other words, what if we introduced each other in ways that gave a sense of our connection to our collective humanity and did not reference our paid work?

Don't get me wrong, I'm not saying money and work are unimportant. It's just that they can quickly become toxic if used as the primary measure of our worth as human beings. No matter what Western culture tells us, money and work *alone* do not create a meaningful life.

This was obvious to the Buddhist king of Bhutan, who, in 1972 when he was just seventeen, bemoaned the widely accepted measurement of productivity, or gross domestic product, as the ultimate marker of a nation's well-being. The wise young monarch declared, "Gross national happiness is more important than gross domestic product," coining both a phrase and a concept that would come to denote Bhutan's more holistic approach to human development. Learning this brings my father's mantra of "Life's mission is to be happy" to mind.

The "Gross National Happiness Index" was eventually implemented by the government of Bhutan as a guideline for economic and social policies. The index recognizes nine domains of well-being—areas of life that policy makers must consider to ensure its people maintain a "good life." Can you imagine if our nation's policy makers were forced to consider measures such as "psychological well-being," "health," "education," and "cultural diversity" when they created new laws, as they must do in Bhutan?

Instead, Western cultures tend to rely on measures of "success" that are rooted in productivity. The problem with this is that there is no end point. For instance, the number of successful operations that "Marc the surgeon" has achieved does not make him a better husband or father. And no matter the size of my annual bonus check, while it gave me momentary joy and comfort, it did not make me sustainably happier. In fact, once it was deposited, I often found myself consumed with wanting an even bigger one the next go-round (hello, Chapter 1's hedonic treadmill).

Welcome to human nature, right? We can't help but think of productivity measurements as being directly tied to our self-worth.

This phenomenon exists in nearly every type of working environment. For example, in academia, very smart individuals are obsessing over Flawed Self-worth Anchors that have little to no bearing on one's true impact as an educator. I'm talking about the "impact factors" or "impact scores" that scholarly journals must now achieve. These "factors" are, essentially, a measurement of the frequency that an average article in that journal has been cited by other articles over a period of time. This ranking system may give you a false sense of the article's worth—and those very authors' worth as researchers and scholars.

"Twenty or thirty years ago, the journals that I published in didn't have an impact factor, they didn't have this number that someone created that allowed people to quantify one publication as opposed to another and compare them," says *The Pricing of Progress* author Dr. Eli Cook, a senior lecturer at Haifa University and a visiting fellow at the Stanford Humanities Center. "And it's crazy now. Like, my entire academic career can be summed up in this one number. . . . Someone created this and then people got sucked in."

On the one hand, Dr. Cook told me, it's a very human tendency to get caught up in Flawed Self-worth Anchors based on nothing more than a clean, simple score. Yet, someone built this idea in order to boost productivity, and soon these rankings become central to the lives of professors and scientists.

"It's like almost the gamification of life," he said. "You have to get these numbers; your life has become like a video game."

Dr. Cook asserts that this is a product of modern culture. In the eighteenth century, he says, Americans anchored their livelihoods and self-worth around something called a "competence."

"Most Americans in the eighteenth century, their idea of what we'd call economic success was that they had enough to feed their families, to live a fairly comfortable lifestyle, and to be free from debt and free from anyone else telling you what to do," Dr. Cook explained to me. "As long as I could put food on the table for my family . . . then that would allow me to be free because I wouldn't have to go work for someone else. That was a very crucial idea in early America."

But today, this historical idea about what constitutes a successful life seems so simplistic to us. The pressure to buy into the Flawed Self-worth Anchors of a productivity-centric culture is so subtle, we often don't even recognize our complicity.

For example, I have a friend whom I have always viewed as "successful." When she was promoted to managing partner at her law firm and named one of the top intellectual property lawyers in the state, I thought, *Wow, how does she do it?* Imagine my surprise when my friend confided to me that, despite outward appearances, internally she feels like she's barely keeping it all together. That she's running on caffeine and anti-anxiety meds, her young children are beginning to prefer the company of their babysitter, and her spouse treats her like a housemate instead of a romantic partner. While feeling completely empathetic to her personal struggles, I also share her story as a reminder of how easy it is for any one of us to define "success" on false terms.

Often, when we say someone is successful, what we're really saying is that they are steadily progressing in their careers, or they live in a big house, or they are always busy. But having a big title, the most stuff, or the fullest calendar doesn't necessarily translate into a full, meaningful life, let alone success.

Take a moment and think about someone you know who is successful. How do you *know*? Is it because they appear to be making a lot of money? Or is it because they have a loving family that enjoys spending time together? Are they successful because they work out every day at 5 a.m. before heading to the office in a power suit? Or is it because they seem to possess strength, clarity, and peace with whatever life brings their way?

Our societal embrace of Flawed Self-worth Anchors has wide-ranging implications. For example, researchers have found that wealthy-*seeming* job applicants often receive unfair advantages. A series of studies conducted in India and the United States sought to determine whether perceived wealth could bestow a halo effect. In one study, subjects were placed in three groups and given superficial details (age, marital status, bank balance, etc.) about a hypothetical person called "Arjun." One group was told that Arjun had 5,000 rupees in the bank (about $65); another was told he had 50 million rupees (more than $645,000); the control group was not given any bank details. All subjects were then asked to rank Arjun's likeliness to "drink tea" or "sleep late" or be "fond of cricket." Scattered within this list of benign rankings were queries about Arjun's presumed confidence, intelligence, and ability to make decisions—all to measure the participants' *perceptions* of Arjun's competence. Across the board, the Arjun with a high bank balance received higher competence rankings than the low-bank-balance Arjun.

The researchers wanted to find out if the halo effect had real-world implications for job-seekers. And in a follow-up study they found that people were also more likely to hire a wealthy applicant than a poor one, even with all qualifications being equal. (Interestingly, if the applicant's wealth had been inherited, all bets were off; the halo effect disappeared. Which goes to show how much we embrace a hard-work ethic.)

Of course, job applicants do not typically share their bank statements. But as the study authors noted, the "cues to wealth" an applicant brings to an interview—such as their home address, an expensive car, or, yes, a four-digit handbag—appear to give them an unfair advantage over applicants with the same skills and abilities.

Have you ever believed that someone was more attractive, likable, or intelligent simply because they possessed the Flawed Self-worth Anchors our culture covets? Did that person turn out to be as compelling and capable as you imagined? Or were they human, fallible, and just trying to measure up, like all of us are, to societal codes around success?

How do you define success for yourself? And how has that definition helped or hurt you in life? Often, we don't even realize we're swept up in a cultural illusion, because our family and our peers have also bought into the false narrative that where you vacation, where your children go to school, what kind of watch you wear, or what kind of purse you carry into a meeting makes you a better person.

FALSE FINANCIAL COMPARISONS

In essence, **False Financial Comparisons** are scenarios in which we believe that the lifestyles of people we perceive as "just like us" are ones that they can afford and therefore we should be able to as well. Maybe they have a nicer car, or a larger flat-screen television, or a better-appointed gourmet kitchen. If comparison to their lifestyle makes us feel bad about ourselves, we are in danger of falling prey to False Financial Comparisons. That's because we don't know if they maxed out their credit cards to pay for those things, took out a second mortgage, or diligently saved little by little to make their purchases. We can only see the result of their spending. In an attempt to mimic their behavior, we can find ourselves going down devastating financial and emotional paths.

In my three decades of helping people make better decisions around money, I've seen how False Financial Comparisons can lead anyone, at any income level—from the minimum-wage worker to the millionaire entrepreneur—to spend way beyond what is reasonable or affordable for them in an attempt to buy their way to a *feeling* of wholeness by "catching up" with others in their social circle. That plan never works.

In my view, three of the most prevalent modern-day forces that have perpetuated our tendency to make False Financial Comparisons are:

1. Easy access to credit
2. Fictional financial lifestyles
3. Social media

Let's take them one at a time.

EASY ACCESS TO CREDIT

Before credit cards and home loans became accessible to a wider swath of Americans, we pretty much lived in and among communities where our neighbors' homes and possessions mirrored ours, because that's what our incomes could bear. Your neighbor owned a single-family home and a used station wagon a lot like yours, because that's all the home and car the bank would allow them to buy.

But then, starting around the early 1980s, the proliferation of **Easy Access to Credit** changed the lifestyles of many U.S. consumers. The widespread introduction of credit cards was a boon for people with sound financial habits, who lived within their means, paid off monthly balances in full, and did not feel the urge to collect Flawed Self-worth Anchors to the point of financial ruin. But this is a lot like saying the introduction of Oreos was a boon to people who can eat just one and put the pack away for another day. Personally, I've never been able to eat just one Oreo.

What made credit cards both enticing and dangerous is that they enabled you for the first time in history to live a lifestyle well beyond your means. Make the minimum monthly payment on your total credit card balance and you were off to the spending races. And the more you used credit for purchases, paying just the minimum each month, the more attractive you were to credit card companies. Soon you'd be getting offers for more cards, with even higher credit limits, because the financial institutions assumed that you'd continue to rack up interest on unpaid balances, which amounted to big profits for them. The math on the interest from unpaid credit card balances over the years is stunning. At an interest rate in the upper teens, making only the minimum payments, you'd ultimately pay nearly twice the purchase cost by the time you paid off that debt.

Additionally, the financial markets became more sophisticated. Banks didn't have to hold your $250,000 home loan on their books anymore; instead they could package it with other mortgages and sell them off as products. Pretty soon you could purchase a house with less than the standard 20 percent down, furnish it with a $25,000-limit credit card, and enjoy your brand-new buy-now, pay-later lifestyle. Next thing you know, your neighbor is upping the lifestyle-creep ante, leasing a new BMW, taking the family to Hawaii, and inviting a hundred people to their daughter's wedding—because "Life Takes Visa," as the company's slogan trumpets.

Of course, not everyone has enjoyed easy access to credit. Tragically, racial and ethnic minorities have historically been hard-pressed to qualify for mortgage and bank loans because of discriminatory lending practices; implicit bias makes it harder for a person of color to secure a job or advance in their chosen profession, which affects their credit access; and predatory payday loans carrying exorbitant fees, interest rates, and penalties have been disproportionately marketed to low-income populations of all backgrounds. Our nation's devastating history of financial discrimination is beyond the scope of this book, but it is important to keep in mind, because it adds yet another layer of hardship for anyone who struggles with the burden of feeling as if they are never enough in a society that tends to affirm that obvious falsehood.

Carl Richards, a certified financial planner, *New York Times* columnist, and author of two personal finance books, is a keen observer of human nature. I asked him why he thinks False Financial Comparisons so easily creep into our lifestyles, even among those of us who believe we are immune to a Never Enough mindset.

"What's so tricky about those words, especially 'enough,' is how insidious and slippery the narratives are," he said. "If you say, 'You're just trying to keep up with the Joneses,' all of us smart, intelligent adults will say, 'No, I don't do that; that's silly. Peer pressure is for teenagers.' But then your neighbor buys a new car. And you don't find yourself thinking, 'I've got to get a new car to one-up the neighbors,' but instead what happens is this subtle little element of *permission* drops into your mind. . . . I don't even think it's conscious. We just think, 'Oh, if it's okay for them, it must be okay for us.'"

Slowly but surely, subtle permission turns into unbearable debt. According to 2021 Experian data, the average American has nearly $96,000 in debt. Where is it focused? The average auto loan balance is nearly $21,000; our personal loans average over $17,000 per person; and for those with mortgage debt, we've seen the highest increase in a decade, with an average balance of $220,000. Then there are student loans, at nearly $40,000 per person; more on those shortly.

It's not that *all* this debt comes from "keeping up with the Joneses." When you dig down deeper into these numbers, you will find real people struggling to pay their bills, keep food on the table and a roof over their heads, and get an education. It's simply to point out that easy access to credit is a cultural practice that can become a very expensive exercise in a world of False Financial Comparisons. We see what our friends and neighbors have. Then we tend to think, as Richards said, "Oh, if it's okay for them, it must be okay for us." So we buy more cars, more houses, and more education than we can afford or even need to live a good life.

One of the most treacherous and widely accepted practices in which Counterfeit Financial Culture runs amok is with our easy access to student loans. A recent *Wall Street Journal* investigation looked at the University of Southern California's online master's in social work program, a two-year, $115,000 online degree, which cost almost the same as the school's in-person classes. The *Journal* found that USC had hired a for-profit company that used aggressive recruiting tactics and flashed the school's prestigious status in order to bolster its enrollment numbers.

However, that degree turned out to have one of the worst combinations of debt to earnings among social work programs among the top colleges, according to U.S. Department of Education data. The *Journal* determined that USC students who took out federal loans to attend the online program borrowed a median of $112,000, and about half of them were earning $52,000 or less per year two years after graduation.

One 2018 graduate said she owed $307,000 in total student loan debt, of which $200,000 went toward her USC degree. She was earning just $48,000 a year as a community mental health therapist in Iowa. "I realize now," she said, "I could have gotten the same job with a much cheaper degree from a different school."

Those who drop out of college, for whatever reasons, risk serious financial devastation. The dropout rate for undergraduate college students in the U.S. is *40 percent*, according to federal data analyzed by the Education Data Initiative. College dropouts are also four times more likely to default on their student loans than non-dropouts. All of this means that the people who suffer most under the weight of student loan debt may also be the same people who never even got their degree.

Economists are also beginning to question the diminishing returns of a college degree that cannot pay for itself. "People didn't use to talk about 'investing in themselves'; that wasn't a phrase that we used to talk about human beings," says Dr. Cook. "But now our whole culture of education is that you *have* to spend all this money to go to college, an enormous amount of money, because you're 'investing in yourself.'"

An education, he adds, is often talked about as "an investment in our job skills." That's the cultural takeaway we all buy into. And while this is absolutely true on many levels, skills training also happens when we get the job. So, in many ways, college becomes more of a "credentialism game": Spend a lot of money or take on an enormous amount of debt to get into a good school, so that when you hit the job market, employers will think: *Oh, she went to a fancy school, so she must be smart.*

"Is it really about going to college?" Dr. Cook noted. "Or is it actually about the race?" He recalls a friend's race to Harvard, which began at his high school: "When someone got into an Ivy League school, the principal would announce it on the loudspeaker. So if you're a fourteen-year-old, a fifteen-year-old, of course, you're going to play this game. That's why we play sports. You're competing with other people. . . . I think it'd be very hard to change that culture."

FICTIONAL FINANCIAL LIFESTYLES

False Financial Comparisons are not limited to people we personally know in real life. Over the past few decades they've even seeped into many of our favorite forms of entertainment. What I'm talking about are the portrayals of lifestyles on TV shows and in movies that simply cannot be achieved based on the career-commensurate incomes presented. I call this phenomenon **Fictional Financial Lifestyles**. Let's take a look at the ones we see on movies and TV.

If you've ever watched the legal TV drama *Suits*, there's a feisty character named Donna whose positive can-do energy I admire. Early in the series, Donna is a legal secretary—and the sharpest-looking one I've ever seen: perfect hair, nails, and exquisite (and exquisitely tailored) clothes. I can't figure out how she pays for all of this. So, I did a back-of-the-envelope calculation of what it would cost to groom like Donna, with daily blowouts, weekly mani-pedis, and a personal shopper. Did I mention that Donna lives in New York City, where the median salary for her position is $65,000, according to job search website Glassdoor? Let's be generous and say that, being an above-average legal secretary, Donna actually earns $75,000. Here's what she would have to spend every year to live in Manhattan and look as amazing as she does:

Weekly mani-pedi: $50 x 52 = $2,600
Weekly workout classes: $25/class x 3 times/week x 52 = $3,900
Twice-a-week blowouts: $50 x 2 x 52 = $5,200
Monthly facials: $125 x 12 = $1,500
Quarterly haircuts and color: $250 x 4 = $1,000
Annual clothing and accessories: $500 x 10 new outfits a year = $5,000

So far, Donna's grooming alone runs her about $19,000 a year—and we haven't yet added in rent, subway and taxi expenses, groceries, utilities, insurance, evenings out with friends, vacations, gifts, charitable contributions, and perhaps student loan debt repayments. But let's be crazy-conservative and say that all of those items add up to just $5,000 a month ($60,000 a year). That brings our grand annual Donna Spending Total to $79,000.

Recall that Donna earns $75,000 a year. In 2021, a person earning

$75,000 in New York City would have paid over $19,000 in federal, state, and local taxes, leaving them with an annual take-home pay of about $56,000.

By my conservative estimates, one would have to make over $100,000 a year before taxes in order to present the same kind of polished New York lifestyle as fictional Donna. In other words, Donna needs to earn 30 percent more than she currently makes to pay for her fabulous life.

Despite my fascination with this character and her personal style, I know that Donna is a financial fantasy. Her ready-for-the-runway hair and perfectly put-together outfits that she wears to overpriced after-work cocktails with colleagues—all of it represents a financial funhouse mirror that does not reflect true dollars-and-cents reality.

Fictional Financial Lifestyles on TV and in the movies have become so common, there's even a website, tvtropes.com, that breaks down some of the most blatant financial falsities for us. Here are a few you may recognize:

- *Friends* **Rent Control** refers to a cast of young, attractive characters who live in enviable homes and apartments that they shouldn't be able to afford given the average salary their characters' jobs would make. This trope is named after the TV show *Friends*, in which the characters (a waitress, chef, masseuse, actor, IT manager, and professor) wave off the obvious disparity in wages to apartment size as "rent control."
- **Pottery Barn Poor** is when the characters are implied to be poor, yet their home is furnished like a beautiful, cozy Pottery Barn showroom. See Mia's apartment in the film *La La Land*.
- **Improbable Food Budgets** are common in shows like *Seinfeld* and *Gilmore Girls*, where the characters are constantly eating at restaurants or ordering takeout, even while some of the characters have low-paying jobs or no job at all.
- **Unlimited Wardrobes** refer to the sorts of gorgeous designer dresses, shoes, and suits worn by the cast of *Sex and the City*,

especially the famously stylish, but poorly paid, columnist Carrie Bradshaw, who was never seen in the same outfit twice.

These characters rarely discuss the nitty-gritty of their work, finances, and money. They rarely, if ever, divulge the size of their paychecks; we are expected to simply suspend our disbelief when Fictional Financial Lifestyles are depicted onscreen. Unfortunately, those depictions have a very real impact on us.

A 2018 study at the London School of Economics found that viewers who consume a steady diet of "materialistic media messages" from TV shows that valorize wealth and fame tend to be more materialistic and less supportive of poor people. Even if study participants were only exposed to very short, sixty-second clips of reality programming such as *Keeping Up with the Kardashians* or *The Apprentice*, it brought about attitudes among participants that tended to be "significantly more materialistic and anti-welfare."

Of course, it can also be great fun to imagine a life like *Suits'* Donna. TV and movies provide a wonderful dose of escapism. But the danger comes for those of us who, deep down, *believe* that we would be more interesting, lovable, and worthy human beings if we also *looked* like Donna on a legal secretary's salary; or dressed as fabulously as Carrie Bradshaw in *Sex and the City* on a writer's wages; or lived in a large, centrally located New York apartment like Rachel's in *Friends*, on a waitress's take-home pay. And so we work harder, take on more debt, and buy into a fantasy.

SOCIAL MEDIA

The late poet Allen Ginsberg once presciently said, "Whoever controls the media, the images, controls the culture." Ginsberg was speaking of traditional media—news, TV, magazines, newspapers. But in the last two decades, the rise of social media has impacted culture in ways we could have never imagined.

Social media platforms like Facebook, Twitter, YouTube, Instagram, and TikTok have opened up our worlds to a global audience, allowing us to peek into the personal lives of friends, learn about the daily experiences of people in far-off countries, or even hang out virtually with celebrities at red carpet events. Social media has also been used by bad actors to manipulate the truth, distort our understanding of world events, and drive a wedge between neighbors. When it comes to the burden of a Never Enough mindset, social media accelerates and exacerbates our worst impulses.

Maybe it's a quiet Saturday evening at home, you pick up your phone and check how many likes you've received on that funny photo of your nephew, and before you know it, you've lost an hour to the Instagram rabbit hole, scrolling down a year's worth of posts on your ex-boyfriend's account (*wow, he seems to be doing better than he deserves*), then his new girlfriend's feed (*how do they have so much time to travel—does she even work?*), then your boss's posts (*she looks amazing in a bathing suit; I should do some sit-ups*). Compare-and-despair scrolling is a tempting, but harmful, use of time for those of us who already suffer feelings of self-doubt.

"I used to look at my ex-girlfriend's Instagram *all* the time," says "Jade," a twenty-one-year-old college student in Los Angeles who told me she scrolls social media for hours, usually at bedtime. "It would start so innocent, like, 'I just want to see what she's up to,' but then I'd be sad and see that she has a whole other life that I don't know anything about."

There's debate in the mental health field about whether "social media addiction" is a true addictive behavior. The fifth edition of the *Diagnostic and Statistical Manual of Mental Disorders* (DSM) only lists "internet gaming disorder" (addiction to video games) as a "condition for further study." But do we really need a psychiatric manual to confirm whether social media has given us a collective FOMO hangover?

For example, several studies have found that social media platforms are actually *designed* to trigger FOMO, or fear of missing out, which itself is associated with increased feelings of stress and anxiety. According to a 2017 report by the United Kingdom's Royal Society for Public Health, social media can be "more addictive than cigarettes and alcohol." Just two hours a day engaging with social media (what's considered "heavy" use) was linked to increased rates of anxiety and depression. As the report's authors note, "The unrealistic expectations set by social media may leave young people with feelings of self-consciousness, low self-esteem, and the pursuit of perfectionism."

Career and workplace expert Lindsey Pollak believes that social media has made our collective striving significantly worse for younger people like Jade.

"As much as you and I grew up wanting to make money and have prestige, what's different now is that there's a tremendous amount of pressure on millennials and Gen Zers to succeed even younger," says Pollak, the author of several bestselling career-advice books. "Manisha, I remember admiring people like Oprah and Suze Orman, who were older and had built a career. But Mark Zuckerberg became *Time*'s Person of the Year at age twenty-six, Greta Thunberg at sixteen. The pressure to succeed young is tremendous. And we didn't have Instagram and LinkedIn and Facebook to show us, every minute of the day, how much more successful other people were."

Even if your life is going really well, Pollak says, "you can always pick up your phone and find somebody going faster, winning more awards, making more money, taking better vacations. That public display of success and wealth, it's always on in the background, and it is really detrimental to the mental health of a lot of young people."

Jade says she tries to keep all this in perspective, using social media primarily as an entertaining distraction. But ultimately, it leads her to feeling anxious about her lifestyle and her finances. "When I see people on TikTok traveling to beautiful places and staying at these really cool Airbnbs while I'm at home in bed? Stuff like that gets me super antsy," she said. "Like, I want to go and do something, but I don't have the money."

Just as the Fictional Financial Lifestyles we see on TV and in movies can have an influence on our materialistic tendencies, social media plies us with another sort of financial envy—except this time, the characters are real people. When a college roommate posts stories from her meal at the cult foodie restaurant The French Laundry on Instagram, or a celebrity influencer raves on YouTube about her expensive, new skin care routine—it's enough to send us straight to retail therapy.

In fact, a 2018 study from Allianz found that nearly 90 percent of millennials say social media has caused them to compare their own wealth and lifestyle to that of their peers (for Gen Xers it was 71 percent; Baby Boomers, 54 percent). A full 57 percent of those millennial respondents say it led them to spend money they weren't planning to. (Guilty. I can't tell you how many antiaging skin care tools I have purchased after scrolling through Instagram, most of which I didn't even know I needed.)

It's crucial to keep in mind that you're never getting the whole story on social media. You don't know, for instance, that your college roommate saved up for six months to pay for that amazing meal at The French Laundry. Or that the celebrity influencer doesn't even use the products she's hawking. In other words, a picture may be worth a thousand words, but if that picture is on social media, it may also be a work of financial fiction.

Jade says that, at heart, she knows that her friends' glamorous snapshots are often a lie, because she's been complicit in a few of her own social media fabrications.

"My roommate and I recently took a trip to Santa Cruz and, first of all, we were horribly hungover, my roommate was crying about some boy, and I was like, I have never felt so horrible I want to die right now," Jade recalls. "Then, when we got to the Airbnb, it was just *un*livable. There were fleas on the bed, hair on the tables, dirt everywhere. But my roommate made this nostalgic little TikTok video about us arriving at this cute Airbnb—and I'm, like, that's not at all what happened!"

o   o   o

It's wonderful to feel inspired to strive for more, to earn more, to be the best version of yourself. But it's crucial that we look beyond the curtain of Counterfeit Financial Culture and ask whether the wealth narratives we are watching play out on TV, in movies, in social media, and among our peers actually reflect financial reality. Privately, we know that self-worth doesn't come from four-digit handbags, or sleek suitcases, or expensive degrees from elite colleges. But as psychotherapist Dr. Kate Levinson reminds us, it can be really hard to hold on to a "less is more" ethos when faced with the "more is more" values of our society.

"I went for a year without buying anything," Dr. Levinson told me. "I bought food, obviously, but I didn't buy clothes, books—I didn't buy *stuff*. I went through withdrawals. It's like breaking an addiction. But if we're always just continuing life as it always is, then we don't get that experience of, '*Oh*, simpler *is* better.'"

Flawed Self-worth Anchors will never make us truly happy, because external symbols of success do not impart a deep sense of self-worth. That feeling can only come from *internal* validation. From knowing: *I am enough*.

Once you begin to experience brief moments in your day when the power of the Hungry Ghost weakens, you may even find yourself exhaling, and feeling joyful and present in your environment, just as it is. That's when you can stop "doing" and savor just "being."

CHAPTER 4

———

~~Do~~ *Be* What You Love

"If I believe that my self-worth and my net worth are the
same, then suddenly this is more than just how much
I made. This is like, how much am I worth?"

As any workaholic will tell you, we love a good to-do list. It used to be that every time I checked a completed task off my list, it delivered a rush of mood-lifting dopamine to my work-addled brain.

So when the *New York Times* recently published the morning to-do list of a Silicon Valley biotech founder, I was mesmerized by the cultish precision of her agenda. Jotted down on a slip of hotel memo paper, this CEO's routine included the following entries:

4:00 a.m.   rise and thank God
4:00–4:15   wash face, change
4:15–4:45   meditate, clear mind
4:45–5:20   work out
5:20–6:20   shower, change, shave, perfect
6:20–6:30   pray
6:30–6:45   breakfast: banana, whey

Not only did she map out her morning to the minute, she also added some no-nonsense affirmations, such as: *I am never a minute late; ALL ABOUT BUSINESS* (yes, it was in all caps); *I am not impulsive; I know the outcome of every encounter; I am always proactive; I am fully present.*

Reading this ambitious morning manifesto, the part of my brain that secretly admires such get-it-done gusto thought: *Look at all she's already accomplished. At 6:45 a.m., she's on her way to the office, while I still have another fifteen minutes before my alarm goes off. There you have it, folks. That's how winners start their day.*

The irony here is that the author of this to-do list was disgraced Theranos founder Elizabeth Holmes, and this note to herself was entered as evidence at her criminal trial.

Holmes was one of the youngest and wealthiest female startup founders in the world before she was charged with defrauding Theranos's investors. She rubbed elbows with tech titans and presidents, graced the covers of numerous magazines, and was named one of *Time*'s "100 Most Influential People" of 2015. A workaholic poster child, Holmes claimed she did not take a single vacation in her twenties, had no friends or life beyond work, and ate a vegan diet because it allowed her to function with less sleep. She convinced reporters, venture capitalists, and even her own employees that Theranos's blood-testing technology was going to change the world. In 2022, thirty-seven-year-old Holmes was convicted of four counts of fraud for lying about a technology that did not even exist.

After being momentarily swept up in her impossible to-do list, I realized that Holmes's story in many ways embodies the destructive myth of Hustle Culture.

Now that we've looked at how personal trauma and Counterfeit Financial Culture can exacerbate a Never Enough mindset, let's examine what happens when those forces collide in the workplace.

"Rise and Grind," "TGIM (Thank God It's Monday)," "you can sleep when you're dead" are just a few rallying cries of Hustle Culture, a movement that worships eighty-plus-hour workweeks, wearing the same thing every day so you can save your brainpower for work-related decisions, and living on meal-replacement shakes because an actual lunch break takes too much time.

Just as the False Financial Comparisons we discussed in Chapter 3 can drive us to #WantItAll, Hustle Culture implores us to #DoItAll—an imperative that's fueled by a heavy dose of employer-driven peer pressure.

Who among us didn't feel shame (or on the flip side, real anger) when Tesla CEO Elon Musk tweeted that "nobody ever changed the world on 40 hours a week." Or when Yahoo's former CEO Marissa Mayer claimed it was possible to work 130 hours a week "if you're strategic about when you sleep, when you shower, and how often you go to the bathroom." I'm embarrassed to admit that my first reaction was: *Brilliant! If I drink less water, I'll need fewer bathroom breaks.*

So how did it come to this? Are eccentric CEOs fueling our tendency toward harmful Never Enough behaviors? Or are we at fault for striving ourselves crazy? Like most things, it's not us-or-them; it's not black-or-white. It's both. It's also more complicated—and darker—than we realize. To start, our own role in working ourselves to death stems, in part, from a gradual cultural shift toward viewing our work as a means to enlightenment.

When *Atlantic* reporter Derek Thompson looked at the last one hundred years of workplace culture, he noticed a fascinating change in our physical and mental devotion to work that coincides with an increased disengagement in organized religion. As Thompson notes, humans like to worship things—whether it's beauty or art or our own children. So as religion became less central to the lives of many Americans, work began to fill that space, and the office became the new house of worship.

"In the past century," Thompson writes, "the American conception of work has shifted from *jobs* to *careers* to *callings*—from necessity to status to meaning. . . . The problem with this gospel—*Your dream job is out there, so never stop hustling*—is that it's a blueprint for spiritual and physical exhaustion."

It's bad enough that our search for meaning at the office often leaves us feeling empty. Now add social media to the mix. "Toil glamour" is how *New York Times* reporter Erin Griffith describes a Hustle Culture in which workers are expected to not only love their jobs, but also to "promote that love on social media, thus fusing their identities to that of their employers."

Then there's "struggle porn," which is how one critic of Hustle Culture describes "a masochistic obsession with pushing yourself harder, listening to people [who] tell you to work harder, and broadcasting to people how hard you're working." I certainly have fallen prey to this kind of pressure, and I suspect many others have, too.

Of course, the Covid pandemic created a seismic shift in the way we view the role work plays in our lives, especially for younger workers. About 37 percent of adults under 30 voluntarily left their jobs in 2021, compared with 17 percent of 30-to-49 year-olds, 9 percent of 50-to-64 year-olds, and 5 percent of workers 65 and older, according to a survey by the Pew Research Center. The top three reasons all of these workers gave for quitting? Low pay, no room for advancement, and "feeling disrespected at work." The last reason, disrespect, is a clear nod to the so-called Great Resignation, which we'll explore shortly. But I would caution against assuming that Covid rendered Hustle Culture dead. Because even as we vow to change our priorities around work and life, deep down we are still Hungry Ghosts, looking to our jobs for personal fulfillment.

Case in point: While 47 percent of respondents in Microsoft's 2022 Work Trend Index say that they were "more likely to put family and personal life over work than they were before the pandemic," their digital footprints tell another story. Studying "trillions of anonymized productivity signals across Microsoft 365" applications, the company compared data from March 2020 to February 2022 and found that the average user *actually* saw their average workday increase by about 13 percent, and they put in 28 percent more after-hours work, and 14 percent more weekend work.

We say that we want to put family and personal life first, but we don't seem to know how. Judging by the number of business books on the best-seller lists promising to teach us how to "do more in less time," it appears we're not so much *rethinking* our relationship to work as we are trying to turn productivity into a peak-performance competition. Even in our downtime, we're listening to podcasts (at 2x speed) while getting in a workout.

Interestingly, in terms of the history of work, obsession with productivity is a fairly new development. Recall, as Dr. Eli Cook pointed out in Chapter 3, that the measure of success for the majority of eighteenth-century Americans revolved around the idea of achieving a basic "competence." The collective mindset was: *If I have enough to feed my family, live a fairly comfortable lifestyle, and be free from debt and being told what to do, I'm living the good life.* Hustling and struggling, measuring our self-worth against our line-item productivity, is *not* how we have historically defined success. Yet the gospel of productivity is a difficult preoccupation to shake, because we've spent decades internalizing it with the help of corporate America . . . and Alexander Hamilton.

In his book *The Pricing of Progress*, Dr. Cook tells an amusing story about the time that U.S. Treasury secretary Hamilton tried to collect economic data on the productivity of manufacturing versus farming. It was 1791, and Hamilton wanted to lobby Congress to give subsidies to manufacturing companies—but first he had to prove that investing in manufacturing provided as much, if not more, bang for the American buck than agriculture. So he wrote to tax collectors across the land and asked them to gather specific economic indicators from local businesses. For example, he told them to ask about the total area of land culled by the lumber company, the number of eggs sold annually by the farmer, and how many people were employed at the silk factory.

Hamilton wanted to ferret out the revenues and costs of various industries so that he could determine the true value of a business. But to his frustration, he discovered that hardly anyone kept details on productivity. The tax collectors could only tell Hamilton that a "great many people" worked at the iron business, the silk manufacturers had "a considerable stock of worm," and trees were cut for timber and fuel with no regard for "lines of property," just as the rancher's cattle seemed to "range at large."

Hamilton's mistake, Dr. Cook writes, is that he "assumed that the American people shared his belief that market productivity trumped other social considerations" when in fact most Americans at that time showed "an almost complete indifference" to compiling statistics around pricing and income. Of course, our once-simpler way of thinking about work and life would soon shift toward Hamilton's worldview, a perspective that Dr. Cook calls "investmentality."

"Investmentality means viewing the world as a capitalized investment," Dr. Cook explained to me. "I look at a human being and, if I own a company, I say to myself, 'Okay, I'm going to invest in this person now, I'm going to pay their salary, and train them. So how much money am I going to get back from them?'"

Through an investmentality lens, we see everything—whether it's trees or real estate or people—as "income-generating units." In other words, if they cost X and they produce Y, how much will they be worth annually?

Today we find investmentality-style analyses everywhere: from the expense of training a new employee (an average of $1,071, according to the most recent 2021 *Training Industry Report*); to the price our economy pays for lost sleep (up to $411 billion a year through tired or absent employees, according to a RAND Europe study); to the average cost of raising a child to age seventeen (about $233,610 for a child born in 2015, according to the most recent report by the U.S. Department of Agriculture, which has been tracking this data since 1960, when the average was $25,230 and parents were mainly concerned with food, housing, and pediatrician visits—not with paying for the latest iPhone, trendy-label clothes, and SAT tutors).

"We're constantly viewing the world in terms of inputs and outputs," Dr. Cook says. "And in many ways, we internalized the idea of investmentality, whereby we began to put a price on human beings."

As terrible as it is to fathom, it can be argued that our tendency to think of humans as capital has seeds rooted in one of the darkest, most abhorrent chapters of American history: slavery.

"Slaveholders in the South talked about the price of their slaves like they talked about the weather," Dr. Cook says. "It would be, 'Oh, I see slave prices are up.' And they would link these prices to questions of productivity. So as slavery became more and more capitalist in the South, and as the industrial revolution became more and more prominent in the North, you're getting this new investmentality, where you begin to view people in a profit-oriented way."

It may seem a real stretch to connect the abject horrors of slavery to modern-day workaholism and Hustle Culture. After all, we are not in literal bondage to our employers, and we are free to quit our jobs, given we accept any financial consequences of that decision. But it's worth reflecting on the fact that many of us have internalized ideas about "human capital." When we use productivity levels to measure our value and worth as human beings, this idea stems in part from the earliest investmentality mindset of racist slaveholders.

As Dr. Cook writes in *The Pricing of Progress*, many of the economic indicators we've come to embrace in modern American capitalism were inspired by the earliest pricing and capitalization analyses around the labor and lives of Black men, women, and children. Among the many examples: In 1706, the editor of a Boston newspaper cited the deaths of forty-four African Americans as generating a "loss to the country" not of *human life* but of "30.1 [British pounds] per head." In 1731, when Benjamin Franklin analyzed the cost of smallpox deaths in Philadelphia, the sixty-four African Americans among the dead were to be valued at the "going price of slaves," never mind whether they may have actually been free. And by 1837, Dr. Cook writes, when "cotton expansion and the internal slave trade had begun to turn slave bodies into capitalized assets that could be bought sold, mortgaged, insured, or securitized," a leading cotton farmer's journal printed a set of measurements to help its readers calculate the costs, capitalization, and depreciation of their slaveholdings. Those calculations were written by Thomas Jefferson.

As Dr. Cook rightly notes, "There is nothing 'natural' about our current obsession with economic indicators." After all, market data can tell us nothing about human thriving, happiness, mental and spiritual well-being—or how we treat one another as human beings. Yet economic indicators have become a central part of how we measure success and everyday life.

So here we are today. Fundamentally, we may understand that our worth and the worth of our peers are not directly tied to how much money we make. Nevertheless, many of us subconsciously believe that the harder we work, the more money we generate, and the more prestige we create, the higher our essential value is to our bosses, our companies, our families—and to ourselves.

Likewise, the Hustle Culture that fuels so much of today's workplace energy springs from investmentality: Overwork now and you'll be rich, successful, and living your best life later. To date, CEOs have not had a strong reason to contradict this kind of thinking. For, as Dr. Cook points out, just as investmentality benefited the bottom lines of slaveholders, Hustle Culture benefits the bottom lines of employers.

Interestingly, he also highlights how *we* are sometimes complicit in this mindset—how employees tend to perpetuate a tacit encouragement of overwork.

"There's an inner group of people and then there's an outer group of people. And if you want to be in this inner group, you've got to show your loyalty with years upon years of hard work," he told me. "And I think that's very interesting because, in many ways, if you look at how capitalism works, the richest people aren't making their money from labor or from hustling; they're making their money because they have assets and those assets are earning returns. So in a world where Elon Musk wakes up in the morning and can be, like, two billion dollars richer, it's interesting to me that there's still a Hustle Culture. Because if you look at where the wealth is coming from, oftentimes it's from buying something for X amount and selling it for Y—it isn't necessarily about hustling."

Dr. Cook says that a rise in the quantification of work is often just a nuanced means of exerting control. Remember those annual bonuses that my colleagues and I would torment ourselves over at the Houston firm? Or even Dr. Cook's preoccupation with the number of articles he needs to publish? "This is the way you get people to work really, really hard," he said. "And if I believe that my self-worth and my net worth are the same, then suddenly this is more than just how much I made. This is like, how much am *I* worth?"

Instead of our historical pursuit of a basic competence, today we live and die by theories of human capital (for example, *your paycheck reflects your worth*), which economists developed in the twentieth century. "Even when we're just talking about how much money we make, it's embedded into the language, the notion that everyone gets what they deserve: 'I *earn* this much,'" Dr. Cook says. "I do think that a lot of people have internalized it."

o   o   o

Productivity is not a measure of my self-worth. I recognize this now. But at the height of my embrace of Hustle Culture, I had so thoroughly internalized the idea deep in the nooks and crannies of my brain that it felt too difficult to detach my very worth as a person from the progress I made (or did not make) on my daily, weekly, monthly, and annual to-do lists.

As a result, I missed out on countless beautiful sunsets, hours of invigorating river kayaking, several special occasions with family, and a multitude of delightful conversations with friends and strangers because I was too focused on hustling.

Back when I worked at the Houston firm, hustling was such a deeply entrenched part of my identity that on one occasion, as I was walking down a hallway, a staff assistant in front of me heard my footsteps and said, without looking back, "I know that's you, Manisha, because you're the only one who *always* walks that fast." I'm embarrassed to admit that, at the time, I took it as a compliment, an acknowledgment of my hard-earned Busy Badge.

By 2014, the year that Elizabeth Holmes graced the cover of *Fortune* magazine (with the ominous headline "This CEO Is Out for Blood"), I was running my own wealth management practice in Santa Fe. I had two employees, both of whom worked remotely, and I was aware enough of the dangers of Hustle Culture to preemptively warn them that I was a bit of a workaholic. They might get emails from me on nights and weekends, I told them, but don't read them until Monday. I truly wanted them to have full lives, encompassing more than work, even though I didn't extend that same grace to myself.

"Craig" was a bright young man in his early thirties who served as my chief operating officer. A captain on his college soccer team, Craig was intellectual, intuitive, and kind. He had a winning combination of a high IQ and plenty of emotional intelligence. Everyone loved Craig, and I trusted him completely. He also had a very gentle, yet effective, way of pointing out my missteps.

Starting my own business was all-consuming, but I'd made it so much harder than it needed to be, and Craig had a front-row seat from which to witness my struggles. I would often call him sobbing after a meeting that I didn't think went well, and he'd give me a pep talk to help me shake off the tears before I headed to my next appointment. He also bore witness to my annoying tendency to sweat over every detail and not move forward on *anything* until it was *perfect*.

For example, I didn't just obsess over every word in the marketing materials that we mailed to potential new clients—I wanted the packaging to be perfect, too. So I researched different shapes and styles of shipping boxes; I found pale, periwinkle-blue tissue paper that perfectly matched the color of our logo; I commissioned the most beautifully designed oval-shaped stickers, embossed with the firm's name, to close the boxes with. When we met with potential new clients, I had an exquisitely formatted checklist (in 12-point Papyrus font) of all the things we needed to know to make sure we understood their situation well enough to decide if we were a fit—and if we were, all the questions I would need to ask in order to manage their finances holistically. Then there were the quarterly reviews of a client's portfolio. This *had* to be the most useful and informative review they'd ever received. Man, did I agonize over our standard operating procedures. I had a three-ring binder that got larger and larger as I tried to document every single step of the process—much in the same way Elizabeth Holmes tried to wrestle her mornings down to the minute.

Craig knew that my switch was always stuck in the "on" position, so he was very excited to share a concept with me that he'd recently heard about at a leadership conference: He asked me to consider the difference between "doing" and "being." The way Craig described it, many of us make the mistake of believing that if we **Do** more (see Chapter 2's Busy Badges) it will bring us all the trappings of a successful life (see Chapter 3's Flawed Self-worth Anchors) so that we will finally **Be** happy. But instead, he said, we should start with who we want to BE: Act in accordance with the kind of human being you want to BE at a soul level, and this will lead you to DO the kinds of things that support your core values and beliefs.

"This may be a concept that could help you," he said with his trademark kindness. This idea was not new to Craig; he already lived from a place of Be. But ever the observer, he could tell from my behavior that this was a completely foreign concept to me. I had always held fast to the magic of Doing. Even as an adolescent, my thinking was: *If I DO all my homework perfectly and earn high marks, I will BE a lovable, worthy human being.* Then my Do changed from "earning high marks" to "earning a high salary."

In fact, most children naturally exist in a place of Be until they start to absorb messages from adults that they should be doing more. Think about it. No child ever gets praised for quiet contemplation. It's not, *Hey, look at you—you're Being!* It's: *Look at you! So productive. You're Doing It!* Even the age-old question we pose to children, *What do you want to be when you grow up?* isn't in search of answers like, "I want to seek the awe in everyday life," or "I want to be kind and curious." What we're really asking is: What career choice will define you?

It's no wonder that by the time we become adults, most of us have lost touch with the practice of Being. Instead we cleave to workplace messaging that tells us, "Do what you love and love what you do!" This cheery admonition, found in countless career self-help books, pushes us to "follow your passion!" and "find a job that you love!" as if work—and not family, relationships, travel, nature, art, hobbies—is the most central experience to our lives. But as the *Atlantic*'s Thompson writes, "Our desks were never meant to be our altars."

"Do What You Love" was also emblazoned on the walls and coffee mugs at WeWork, the cultish coworking startup that suffered major reputational and economic setbacks due to the financial missteps of its eccentric former CEO. WeWork sought to erase the boundaries between work and life. Even its mission, "To create a world where people work to make a life, not just a living," implored us to find greater meaning at the office, which, when you think about it, is a rather elitist idea: Do *all* jobs have to be life-changing and rapturous? Sometimes a job is just a paycheck.

As the journalist Sarah Jaffe observes in her book *Work Won't Love You Back*, we've grown so accustomed to believing that work brings us meaning and fulfillment that "saying otherwise is an act of rebellion." But love, as Jaffe notes, doesn't come from a job. It's a bond we share with other people. When you choose to Be more and Do less, it frees you from having to Do What You Love for a living—and then spending all your time proving to your employer how much you love your job by hustling at it.

Granted, shifting toward a *Be* What You Love mindset might mean reassessing some of life's biggest decisions. How might it color your perceptions of money and work if you focused on who you want to Be in life, rather than what you will Do? Would you still join the family business? Start your own company? Consider working abroad even if it's for less money? Would you go to college, or graduate school? Or go straight into work to learn a new trade? Would you build products that make you the most amount of money? Or would you find work that provides a basic competence, giving you the freedom to be the kind of person you want to be?

It's hard to simply Be when our workplace culture hive-minds us around the idea that our worth is tied to our productivity. Many of us have internalized Hustle Culture to the point where we are terribly uncomfortable when we're not Doing. I can think of many notable entrepreneurs and CEOs in intense industries who get so wrapped up in Do energy that they feel completely off-kilter when they try on Be. Some resort to wellness gurus and trendy fads—like seven-day fasts, arctic ice baths, and ayahuasca odysseys with shamans—in an effort to kick-start the *feeling* of presence. Many more of us find that we are so fixated on achieving, when we finally catch the things we're pursuing, it still doesn't bring us peace.

"My experience with accomplishments is that they kind of overpromise and underdeliver," Scott Kriens, the chairman and former CEO of tech giant Juniper Networks, said when I interviewed him for the *True Wellth* podcast in 2019. "There's the promise that it'll be some sense of deep peace, and it isn't—it's just another thing before the next thing and after the last thing, and it's not *the* thing."

In 2010, Kriens and his wife, Joanie, started the 1440 Foundation, an organization committed to the cultivation of authentic and connected relationships as a basis for living well. They next launched 1440 Multiversity, an educational retreat in the California redwoods of Santa Cruz. Kriens is *deeply* committed to learning and building. Yet he admits that one of his biggest challenges in life is the struggle of *doing* enough.

"You could pick for me, in my life, any number of things that I've had the great good fortune to be part of," he said. "And each time, if I'm really brutally honest about it, somewhere in my mind, I was thinking, 'Well once you've done *this*, then you will have arrived.' Instead of that being what happened . . . it just led to the question, 'Well, *now* what do I need to make me happy?'"

Doing versus Being is a dilemma that can affect all of us, no matter our path in life or our work situation. I know a custom cabinetmaker who does absolutely impeccable woodwork. He loves his craft and the panache that comes from being known throughout the state as the best of the best. But on the flip side, he lives at his shop seven days a week. His wife and kids visit him there. He's in poor health and is missing moments with his family, because for him, Doing always takes precedence.

It's not that our work shouldn't bring us pleasure. When I'm helping women find greater security and personal power, I genuinely love what I am doing. But I have also learned to value the *longer-lasting* contentment of being present, living with integrity, and spending time with the people, causes, and hobbies that matter most to me. When we make time for both the Doing and Being facets of life, we not only engage more meaningfully with both of these practices, we experience more joy in life overall.

That's where the pandemic, as terrible as it has been, brought a silver lining: It forced many of us to rethink our Doing to Being ratio. When coronavirus swept the globe in 2020 and upended our lives, those of us who had the privilege to switch to remote work were given a unique opportunity to reflect on why we were hustling in the first place. And millions of people around the world began quitting their jobs—at record rates.

In the United States, 4.5 million Americans left their jobs in November 2021, an all-time high. In China, where younger workers grew disenchanted with low wages and "996" schedules—a reference to the grueling expectation that one should work 9 a.m. to 9 p.m., six days a week—many vowed to "lie flat," opting out of work altogether. In Germany, a survey by the IFO Institute found that one-third of all companies were experiencing a scarcity of skilled workers. A Microsoft study of more than 30,000 people in thirty-one countries found that more than 40 percent of the global workforce was considering leaving their jobs in 2021.

For the first time, maybe ever, burnout and overwork weren't seen as *just* employee problems—something that *we* had to wrestle with as we sought out ever-greater reservoirs of grit and perseverance in the face of mounting pressure to #HustleHarder. Now companies had to reckon with a shortage of workers. The Great Resignation forced many CEOs to ask: What can we do to attract and retain staff?

Instead of resorting to the usual Hustle Culture enticements of pay raises and bonuses, some companies granted time off that wasn't attached to an employee's productivity levels. For example, the dating app Bumble gave its employees a full week of paid leave in June 2022, and then made that extra week of paid vacation a permanent benefit for all of its employees. LinkedIn gave its workers a week of paid time off in April 2021 to fight burnout, in addition to the full week they already receive at year's end. And Citigroup investment bank instituted Zoom-free Fridays and designated May 28 a paid holiday that CEO Jane Fraser dubbed "Citi Reset Day."

On the flip side, in 2023 we saw a slew of large tech companies lay off thousands of employees, including people who'd worked at these firms for decades. Shockingly, many termination notices were delivered via cold, impersonal emails. It's no wonder that so many of us are questioning our loyalty to our jobs and the role that work plays in our lives.

"It's a really interesting moment, and I think it could be a turning point, in the sense that people just aren't willing to do Hustle Culture anymore," Dr. Cook says. "If I were a businessman, the thing that would worry me most about the pandemic would be *that*. Will the pandemic create cultural changes that reprogram our values in a way that, suddenly, those bonuses and the rat race don't seem as attractive anymore?"

I asked this question of my friend and author Cali Williams Yost, the CEO and founder of the Flex+Strategy Group. "I do think the workplace has been changed by Covid and that we are *not* going back to how it was, if people choose to leverage that," she told me. "But no organization will come to you and say, 'Hey, you, what do you need?' They can say, 'Yes, we will support this idea you're bringing to us,' but you are the one who needs to come to the table and say, 'This is what I need.'"

As a flexible workplace strategist, futurist, and trend-spotter, Yost helps individuals, corporations, and institutions (which have included Con Edison, UBS Americas, the National Institutes of Health, the United Nations, Columbia University, and many more) determine how to best answer the question: *What do we need to get done, and how, when, and where do we do it best?* Sometimes that means transforming a nine-to-five culture into a more responsive infrastructure that allows employees to do remote work, flex hours, reduced hours—whatever flexible work plan is best for that specific person and the role that needs to be filled—as a way to retain talent.

Yost coined the phrase "work+life fit" more than twenty years ago as a positive counterpoint to the concept of "work-life balance." She found that asking for more work-life fit helped to neutralize the tendency of bosses to translate a request for more work-life balance into a de facto "I want to work *less.*"

"Work-life balance does not exist," she said. "It's a deficit model, and something you're never going to get. Whereas work-life fit is all about the possibilities. It acknowledges the fact that we're all different—there's no two work-life fit realities—and it's something that changes and that you can manage."

While the pandemic has opened the door for us to be more creative about work-life fit, Yost asserts that we must first take a hard look in the mirror and decide what we truly want.

"What I've observed," Yost said, "is that unless people redefine what success means to them personally, they might shift their work hours in an optimal way so they get more time at home, but then they feel bad when they don't get promoted as quickly, or they miss a big meeting, or they're making less money."

Yost was describing my experience perfectly. Each time I had decided I was going to Do less and Be more, I ended up feeling terrible, knowing that I was not making as much money as I used to. Whenever I would choose to lessen my workload, I'd get a pang of envy when I read about a former colleague's big promotion. As Yost explains, you can't change the underlying behavior if you don't first redefine what's most important to you.

Yost counsels us to "redefine success" by considering priorities in four specific realms:

1. Caregiving
2. Prestige
3. Money
4. Advancement

These are the four big buckets that her clients tend to lean into when they are thinking about what success looks like.

Keep in mind that these four words mean different things to different people, and your ideas around them will be unique to your situation. For example, you might decide that having a healthy, enduring connection to family and community is the height of success, which means your work-life fit plan requires that you devote more of yourself to Caregiving, and less to making Money. Or, if Prestige is absolutely central to your definition of success, maybe you take a lower-paying job (less Money) that gives you more time to spend on writing that bestselling book (more Prestige). Or if making partner at the firm is your measure of success, you may want to hold off on starting a family or doing volunteer work (less Caregiving) until you feel like you've been promoted (more Advancement) to a work role and title that satisfies you.

When I asked Yost to describe her steps one by one, she relayed the story of a friend, a high-achieving working mother in the financial services industry who was pregnant with her third child when Yost happened to run into her.

"I asked, 'How are things going?' and she burst into tears, told me she couldn't do it anymore, and was quitting her job," said Yost, who convinced her friend to hold off on handing over a resignation letter to her boss, and instead devise a better work-life fit strategy.

The next morning, they met at a coffee shop, and Yost helped her friend to first redefine success. She determined that Caregiving was her new top priority: She wanted to fit in more time with her growing family. Next, the two of them came up with a proposal she would present to her supervisor, which reduced her work to four days a week, with one of those days being remote.

Then, as they were writing the proposal, Yost had to occasionally remind her friend what "success" looked like now. For example, when she still wanted to keep all of her high-profile responsibilities, Yost told her, "That's not going to work. You've got to give away some of the good things. You have to be okay with the fact that you are going to have less Prestige and you will be making less Money. But now you can redefine success in relation to your kids, because part of why you are doing this is that you want to be there for them."

Her friend agreed. Of course, that was what she wanted. She was certain of it. But she was very uncertain if her boss would accept her new terms when she presented her plan—her final step.

"She kept saying to me, 'Cali, they're never going to go for it,'" Yost recalls. "I said, 'Okay, but maybe they will. The worst they can do is say no.'"

The next day, her friend called and said, "I'm so mad, I didn't even get a chance to present my proposal. I just walked in and my boss said, 'Whatever you want, it's fine.'"

"So many moms do not advance or they drop out of the workforce altogether, when maybe what they need to do instead is take a step back in their jobs," Yost says. "But we live in a world in which stepping back is perceived as a terrible thing—that it's better to quit than move into the slower lane."

Yost's friend worked in the slower lane for almost two years. Then she redefined success again after her marketing executive husband decided that he wanted to become a teacher. She realized she really wanted to go back to work full-time. So, they switched lanes! She refocused on Money and Advancement and he got to be the primary Caregiver, home in time at the end of every workday to hang out with their kids.

Yost often finds that the employees of her corporate clients are more resistant to the idea of flexible work than their employers are. "I cannot tell you the number of times, over the years, that managers have said to me: 'I was one hundred percent fine with this person working remotely, two or three days a week, or reducing their schedule. I wish they would've said something, we would've worked it out,'" she says.

But she also acknowledges that many employers have still not connected the dots to see how strategic work-flexibility practices can create a burgeoning bottom line. Nor have societal norms around work and Caregiving progressed to the point where we support workers who'd like to reshuffle their priorities. The narrative is still: "A parent steps back and they are forever consigned to 'she's not serious; he's not serious,'" Yost says. "We all have to make room for parents to be able to say, 'Right now, I just need to recalibrate this for myself. What could I do? What does that look like?'"

Here's what I take away from Yost's insights:

First, *you* have to redefine what success means to you. Imagine how you could fit your work and life together differently in order to focus on the realm of success you care about most right now—not in three or five or ten years. And as you redefine success, give yourself permission to do less. Try to avoid black-or-white judgments—*there's only one path; I am all in or I quit*—which don't allow you to think creatively about your path.

Second, be okay with the slower lane if that's what you've chosen for now. "No, you don't have to advance all the time. No, you do not have to worry if you've missed that meeting. No, it's okay you didn't make the cupcakes for the class party," Yost reminds us. "What matters to you? Are you content right now? Does this work-life fit work for you? If it does, that's enough." Or as author Elizabeth Gilbert memorably put it, "You are not a Fortune 500 company. You don't have to show increasing profits."

Of course, like most pieces of sage wisdom, in real life it's often difficult to digest. When I first thought about what it would look like to "redefine success," I was tempted to throw all my eggs in the *Money! Prestige! Advancement!* baskets of professional life. But I know that this mindset does not serve me well. At this stage of my life, my gut is loudly telling me that success looks like a blend of Caregiving, which, for me, means being connected to my family, myself, my community, and the people and experiences that matter most to me; and Advancement, which I now define as the pursuit of knowledge and new skills that often have nothing to do with work—things like stand-up paddleboard yoga, fixing things around the house, learning more about nutrition. This combination feels true to my soul.

Don't get me wrong: I still like making Money. I like it a lot. But what I like more is the freedom money gives me to spend my time in ways that make me happy.

Simply doing this exercise, redefining success, will start to change the way you see the world. You may begin to notice other people redefining success for themselves, and wonder how it's working for them. As I write this, I'm inspired by tennis star Ash Barty's announcement that she was retiring from competing, at age twenty-five, while she was still number one in the world and the reigning Wimbledon champion.

"I'm so happy, and I'm so ready, and I just know at the moment, in my heart, for me as a person this is right," she said. "[Tennis] has given me all of my dreams possible, but I know that the time is right now for me to step away and chase other dreams."

To step away from the Money and Prestige—especially when there was plenty left on the table—is astonishing and admirable. Why did she do it? To put it simply: She redefined her definition of success. And it no longer involved giving all her time and energy to the tour.

"There was a perspective shift in me in this second phase of my career that my happiness wasn't dependent on the results. And success for me is knowing that I've given absolutely everything I can," she said. "I know that people may not understand it and that's okay. I'm okay with that."

What if she decides she misses the court, and wants to go back to the rackets? That would be fine. After all, even football star Tom Brady is allowed to change his mind about retirement now and then, and again, and one more time. Yost tells me that everyone, no matter their work journey, is worthy of a "reset." We can rethink our work-life fit and tweak it as many times as we want.

"There are no limits," she says. "But it's a skill set we need to learn. Because when that moment of reset comes, how do you think it through? What are the signs that you need to change things up?"

That last question may be the most vital of all. For a lot of people, unfortunately, a reset happens *to* them before they've had the opportunity to think it through.

"Maybe you get sick, or somebody you love gets sick, or you want to go back to school, or you want to retire. Those tend to be the big moments," she says. "The hope is that you don't have to get to a point of tragedy to make a reset."

When I look back on my own resets, Yost's words ring true. My first reset occurred when I left the Houston firm: I did it impulsively without thought to what really needed to change in my life to make work truly work for me. Because I hadn't defined success, I ping-ponged for quite some time, writing books and doing media appearances (*Prestige*), giving keynote speeches (*Money*), and finally, opening my own financial advisory practice (*Money, Prestige, and Advancement, all in one wrapper!*). I was on a nonstop, joyless quest to do anything it would take to fill all three buckets to the brim.

Another big reset came at the end of 2014, when I merged my private practice with a much larger wealth management firm.

"But you had to get to a point of illness before you took that step, isn't that right?" Yost asked.

"Yes," I said. She was right. I became terribly ill and ended up in the hospital.

"And when you recovered and went to work for the larger firm," Yost asked, "did you redefine success for yourself in order to make that work?"

"No," I said. "I didn't."

o o o

When we consider the many complex factors that contribute to and perpetuate our harmful workaholic behaviors—from the personal (small-*t* traumas), to the societal (living in a world awash in Counterfeit Financial Culture) to the workplace (experiencing the land of Hustle Culture and

Busy Badges)—it can feel almost impossible to overcome the urge to Do more. But these painful narratives do not define us. Our productivity does not indicate our value as human beings. This was something that I had to remind myself again and again and again.

Today, I can see with clarity that when I didn't pause, breathe, and redefine success for myself, I just kept running into the same wall. Even though I thought I was slowing down, I *still* struggled with thinking that I wasn't doing enough.

That kind of thinking surely contributed to the ending of my marriage in 2015. For the life of me, I could not be present with my then-husband. The answer to everything, I was certain, was to work harder. Head down, power through, push myself just a little *more*. Do, Do, DO. When I carried that energy into my next major life reset, it almost killed me.

CHAPTER 5

Hardwired to Hustle

"If we are to understand anything so complex and troubling as addiction, we need to gaze directly at the point where experience and biology meet."

At the end of 2015, after my divorce, I moved to Portland, Oregon, and *vowed* to spend more time Being. In fact, I chose Portland as a kind of soft-landing spot because it is the home of some of the country's best third-wave coffeehouses. I've found that one of the greatest small joys in my life is a good, independent, artsy coffee shop, where I will easily spend three hours nursing a hand-crafted cold brew, while doing work or chatting with a friend.

By early 2018, I had the opportunity to take on a larger role as a national thought-leader for a wealth management firm based in Seattle, Washington. The cofounders who ran the firm were savvy and supportive. My teammates were wise and welcoming. I had the privilege of working with some of the best people I'd ever known.

Yet I still hadn't figured out what success looked like for me. So I dived into my new position, operating with the same frenetic hustle energy of my youth. As a result, by the summer of 2019, I came down with a mysterious illness that finally forced me to begin rethinking how I wanted to spend the rest of my life. In terms of resets, it was quite literally a change-or-die moment.

It all started with brain-numbing fatigue. From my drooping eyelids down to my shuffling feet, every muscle and bone felt like deadweight. It was impossible to hide my condition; I traveled twice a month from Portland to the Seattle headquarters to speak at client events, tape podcast interviews, and brainstorm with the marketing team. Every afternoon, I'd stumble to the wellness room reserved for nursing mothers, curl up in a ball, and fall asleep until the alarm on my phone alerted me to the next essential work commitment. Returning to my hotel each night, I'd collapse into bed. On a typical Seattle workday, I was awake for eight hours and out cold for the other sixteen.

By August, my fatigue was joined by a stubborn 101-degree fever and patchy, red welts across my body and scalp—swollen rashes that hurt to touch. Concerned, my primary care physician ordered some initial blood tests, including one that measured my erythrocyte sedimentation rate, or sed rate, a number that would tell her the level of inflammatory activity in my body.

According to the Mayo Clinic, a normal sed rate for women is in the 0–22 range. Mine clocked in at 95. My doctor explained that an elevated sed rate could certainly explain the rashes, fever, and fatigue: My immune system was revved up and fighting. But *what,* exactly?

My physician sent me to the hospital for a battery of lab work. I still remember the startled expression on the phlebotomist's face when he reviewed my chart and blurted out, "Wow, this is a *lot* of tests. Wonder what's wrong with you?" and I promptly burst into tears.

What *was* wrong with me? When I asked Dr. Google about my problem (rarely a good idea), I learned that a sed rate above 100 could indicate inflammation caused by active disease—potentially cancer, blood conditions, heart disease, and other terrifying scenarios.

Looking back on that period of my life, I was petrified at the thought of losing my health. But if I'm being honest, I was equally afraid of losing momentum at work. I had a new podcast launching, media appearances lined up, and nonprofit board work to attend to. I didn't have time to get sick. Yet, I knew the risks of my obsession, because I had been down this road before, five years earlier . . .

In 2014, on the last day of a motorcycling trip in Laos with my then-husband, I was at an outdoor café, so involved in my laptop that I forgot to reapply bug spray and became easy prey for a mosquito that would almost cost me my life. About a week later, while I was giving a speech in Texas, a bone-crushing pain came over my body and my head felt like it was being squeezed in a vise. I have zero recollection of leaving the conference, driving my rental car back to the airport, getting on the plane, and then making the hour-long drive from the airport in Albuquerque to my home in Santa Fe. Thankfully, my then-husband took me straight to the emergency room. After a litany of tests, including blood draws, CT scans, and MRIs, the doctors informed me that I had contracted dengue fever, a potentially fatal tropical virus.

Severe dengue such as I was experiencing can cause persistent vomiting, internal bleeding, organ failure, and shock as your blood pressure plummets. To date, there is no pharmaceutical cure, merely supportive hospital care, IV fluids, and pain meds until your body can eradicate the virus from your system. But my symptoms only worsened at the hospital. I developed a dangerously high 104-degree fever; chills so strong, my teeth chattered with a force I never knew possible; bones that hurt to such a degree that I was put on morphine; and oxygenation levels that had plunged so low, I was quite literally gasping for air.

My parents and my brother flew in from across the country because the doctors were uncertain if I would make it. Seeing my family gathered around my bedside, I discovered that the old cliché is absolutely spot-on: No one ever lies on their deathbed thinking, *I wish I had worked more.* All I could think about were the people I loved. Could I have done things any differently? Made a more positive contribution to their lives and the lives of others? In those critical few hours when none of us knew whether I would survive, I saw clearly what really matters in the end.

This moment should have marked a turning point in my struggle. But the minute I felt strong enough for a real conversation, I asked my assistant to come to the hospital and we devised a game plan that enabled me to work while on doctor-ordered bedrest during what became a three-month recuperation.

Surviving dengue fever was my first change-or-die moment. Now here I was again, five years later in the summer of 2019, sick with who-knows-what, and moving in a feverish stupor from the bed to the sofa and back, trying to compose emails and push myself just a *little harder*. Never enough. At one point, I fell asleep in the middle of a board conference call. I don't know how long I was out or if anyone called my name, but I woke up hours after the call ended to silence on the line.

By September 2019, shortly after my forty-ninth birthday, my physician came to a diagnosis: hyperinflammation of unknown origin accompanied by acute Epstein-Barr. As she explained it, years of stress-induced cortisol constantly pumping through my body had not only made it impossible for my immune system to efficiently fend off the Epstein-Barr virus but also appeared to now be causing my body to start attacking itself. Normally upbeat and cheerful, my physician was serious and somber when she told me that my numbers were not getting better, that I was not going to power through this time, and that if I didn't rest—in bed, with absolutely no work—my condition was only going to worsen.

Just the thought of not working filled me with terror. Who was I without my work?

Still, exhausted and completely beaten down by illness, I had no choice but to acquiesce. With a pit in my stomach, I asked my bosses if I could take a four-month leave of absence. Everyone at the firm was so supportive, it made me feel . . . well, even worse, frankly. I felt like I'd failed them.

For the first few months of leave, I slept more hours than I was awake as my body went into forced hibernation so it could heal. When I was awake, the most I could do was consume bowls of warm tomato soup while binge-watching crime dramas and take the occasional hot shower. Much to my surprise, as the months passed in slow motion, I started to gain a sense of comfort with just being present—a state of mind I'd never experienced before.

One day during my convalescence, I looked up from the sofa and noticed a framed print perched on a shelf directly above my desk. Drawn with a Sharpie, it was a sketch of a triangle with the words *simplicity* at the top, *small joys* in the lower left, and *financial independence* in the lower right. This visual depiction of my personal mantra was handcrafted by my dear friend Carl Richards, who for more than a decade was a *New York Times* financial columnist known as the "Sketch Guy." I kept it in a prominent place as a reminder of one of the happiest times in my life—my junior year of college.

My mind drifted to the time at twenty years old, when I had the magical experience of studying abroad at Oxford, a historic medieval university in England. I spent my days roaming cobblestone streets, admiring the architecture, and researching and writing in magnificent, dark-wood-paneled libraries. Oxford was where I first read Virginia Woolf's *A Room of One's Own*, in which Woolf asserts that to be able to write, a woman needs money and a solitary space of her own. It was the first time I'd considered that we need financial freedom in order to pursue intellectual freedom. It reminded me of what my mother had taught me over the years—that money gives women voices and choices.

Importantly, I also learned that achieving a sense of freedom did not require buckets of money. At the time, the things that brought me the greatest joy were not expensive. During term breaks, I traveled through Europe on the proverbial twenty dollars a day (this was back in 1991 dollars, to be fair), experiencing a food-lover's dream. I toured iconic Italian cities, where I indulged (daily) in the best gelato I'd ever tasted.

I meandered the Left Bank in Paris and ate decadent almond croissants, the kind where the marzipan-like almond paste oozes out the sides with every bite. After the academic year ended, I spent the summer teaching English to bright young girls in the idyllic waterfront city of Vigo, on the western coast of Spain, where I indulged in fresh, grilled *pulpo* (octopus) and *churros con chocolate* (a fried donut-like treat served with a small cup of dark, dense drinking chocolate). I love to eat.

On the plane ride home after that glorious year abroad, I wanted to keep the memories and feelings I'd experienced close. So, I came up with my triangle mantra to serve as a visual representation of what I felt were to be my life's goals: *simplicity, small joys, financial independence.* I wrote it out on a cocktail napkin right there on the plane.

"This," I had said to myself, "is what I want my life to be driven by."

It's a very human tendency to declare your vision, and then not actually follow it.

Fast-forward to age forty-nine: I had financial independence, but nothing in my life was simple, and my days of wandering in search of small joys had dwindled to zero. Thinking back on this incredibly special year, it pained me to discover how far off course I'd gone.

But then something interesting happened. Instead of beating myself up for my failures, I let my mind drift, and asked, *What small joys make me happy right now?*

I didn't even have to think about it, the answers came so fast: these clean flannel pajamas. I love how, when I first put them on, I can still smell fabric softener. And this microfiber blanket is just so snuggly. Oh, and if I put lotion on the bottom of my feet, then put the blanket over and just rub my feet together, like this, it feels so good.

My mood began to lift just thinking about these small joys.

Recovery from Epstein-Barr took longer than expected. But after another few months, my energy finally started to improve enough to walk the three blocks from my condo to Courier Coffee, a cozy Portland institution with beautiful old floor-to-ceiling windows. Feeling the sunlight streaming through the glass, smelling the freshly ground beans, holding the warm, white mug, listening to snippets of conversations—it was a sensory smorgasbord.

This is what I love. I thought to myself: *Just like my summer abroad—none of this joy requires tons of money. So why am I killing myself chasing after more? I already have what makes me happy right now.*

By March 2020, I was feeling strong again. Seven months had passed since I'd asked for a four-month leave of absence. When my sed rate finally dropped below 20, my doctor gave me the all-clear to go back to work—albeit with a stern reminder: If I shook my life up vigorously via continued workaholism, I most likely would get sick again, but worse. (I've since come to learn just how much worse. In 2022, scientists at Harvard studied more than 10 million young adults and found that Epstein-Barr was likely a causal factor for multiple sclerosis, a chronic disease that triggers the immune system to attack the brain and spinal cord, potentially leading to memory problems, pain, fatigue, numbness, blindness, and paralysis.)

Here is where I would love to report that I learned my lesson and heeded my doctor's orders. That I took lunches on a blanket in the park, shut down my computer on Friday night, and did not turn it back on again until Monday morning. But that is not at *all* what happened. Within three months, I was once again full-speed-ahead Manisha.

This time, at least, I had the presence of mind to acknowledge defeat. I hated that my day started and ended with a phone in my hands, checking and responding to endless emails and texts. I didn't like that when I reflected back on the week, it was a blur of Zoom calls, PowerPoint slides, and Google Docs. Or that weekends were spent hunkering down and "catching up" for the week ahead.

Simply acknowledging that my addiction was fatal to my relationships and to my health didn't seem to change my behavior one bit. I'd add yet another Zoom meeting to my already jam-packed calendar, and some part of me would think: *Here we go again. This time, I really am going to kill myself.*

o o o

A smart friend once said to me, "Honey, I love you, but it's not like you're a brain surgeon. You're not saving the world with your work. So get over it and go have a life."

I loved her for saying that. *Yeah*, I thought, *why* am I *still doing this? Why must I say yes to all the things?* But I felt powerless to just get over it and go have a life. And until recently, I wasn't sure why.

As we've now seen, personal traumas can push us toward extreme busyness; Counterfeit Financial Culture can plunge us into the depths of want-more-do-more mania; and the myth of Hustle Culture can whip up a lot of peer-pressured, employer-sanctioned burnout.

But why is it that very intelligent human beings can recognize these influences, acknowledge that a toxic obsession with work, money, and prestige is deadly, and yet still toil to the brink of death? Recall the stories from Chapter 1, of people like Jonathan Frostick, who wanted to re-schedule his heart attack, or Sara McElroy, who put off medical treatment because she'd just been promoted. Or my own experiences enduring the collapse of my health, twice, only to return to my workhorse ways both times. If workaholism is an addiction, then we are the faces of relapse.

All of this made me wonder: Maybe there's something else? Another piece of the puzzle that makes it so hard to step away from our desks. Could a preoccupation with never-ending goals have deeper biological underpinnings? Because in the times when I have been in the throes of work, it's as if I'm on a runaway train that's about to jump the tracks and crash and there is nothing I can do to stop it.

I called Dr. Rebecca Heiss, an evolutionary biologist and stress physiologist, to see if she could help me unpack this workaholic's dilemma.

"It sounds like you're pulling at the biological, instinctual, and evolutionary factors that contribute to your problem," Dr. Heiss said, "and I think workaholism is a great example of a runaway trait."

Dr. Heiss is an author and sought-after speaker whose early research has been called "transformative" by the National Science Foundation. In her book *Instinct*, she explores self-sabotaging behaviors that spring from our primitive imperatives—those instincts that were once crucial to our ancestors' survival but are now leading us astray. For example, while it was once vital to our survival that we be wary of strangers (after all, they might steal our food and our mates), today that same "fear of others" breeds intolerance, racism, and troubling behaviors that don't match the reality on the ground (for example, the person who doesn't look like a member of your "tribe" is not necessarily out to steal your food or shelter).

Likewise, Dr. Heiss said, "working really hard was a great trait to have in a dangerous, primitive environment, because you'd have access to more resources, gain the respect of your tribe, and achieve a higher social ranking."

From an evolutionary perspective, social standing was *everything* to our ancestors, Dr. Heiss explains, because getting exiled from your tribe was a death sentence. There were just too many dangers (saber-toothed tigers, starvation, lack of shelter) for one to manage alone. As a result, our brains are hardwired to fear rejection, isolation, bad reviews—anything that may have put our ancestors' survival at risk.

These traits apply to our work habits, as well. A steady Stone Age provider had limited hours in the day during which she could hunt, forage, and perform her tribal duties. But today's workaholic can toil *all* the time if she wants to—which is problematic, as Dr. Heiss points out, because it creates the conditions for a runaway trait. As a result, the very thing that all that laboring was meant to do—secure our bonds to our clan—is now *keeping* us from developing those bonds.

"From a biological perspective, our primitive brains push us to work hard to get those social connections—but in fact, when you're a workaholic, you're actually limiting yourself from having them because you choose work over relationships," Dr. Heiss says. "But let me be really clear. There's a difference between operating out of fear versus operating from a sense of purpose and a drive for that purpose. Workaholics have gotten into a space where they're operating from fear."

Learning that there's a potential biological angle to Never Enough-ism feels incredibly empowering. Like, if we can just take control of this runaway trait, if we can hack those tired old neural patterns, maybe there's hope.

Dr. Heiss suggests that workaholics reflect on our behavior in terms our brains can understand. Specifically, identifying both the triggering events that cause us **fear and pain**, and the soothing behaviors that bring us **pleasure and rewards**. Develop clarity around these twin forces, she argues, and you can begin to unpack how they play a role in the runaway traits that you want to rein in.

I know that, for me, many of those **fear and pain** triggers began in grade school when I was repeatedly rejected by my peers. This is mortifying for me to admit. I'm a middle-aged woman, so how on earth can something that happened forty years ago still be influencing my behavior today?

"The brain's not fully mature until age twenty-five or so," Dr. Heiss says, "so those early 'little-*t* traumas,' or microtraumas, can have a massive impact on the brain."

Again, for many workaholics, our little-*t* traumas did not rise to the level of severe harm or physical abuse. However, just being dismissed or ignored by our peers or our parents during our formative years can get rooted in our brain's operating systems. It registers as a **painful** personal attack. So much so that our survival-obsessed brain responds with intense **fear**: *I must prove my worth to anyone who will accept me*—which, for me, turned out to be my teachers, my college professors, and later, my bosses. But then, on the flip side, I also received **pleasure and rewards** from achieving good grades, making money for my firm and for myself, and being told what a hard worker I was.

This combination of avoiding pain and receiving rewards creates strong behavioral patterns. As Dr. Heiss describes it, "If you tell a kid to work hard and then they get rewarded for it, that's altering her neural pathways. Her brain responds with *This feels good. I need to work harder. And if I just work hard, then I get that dopamine hit.* You establish these behavioral patterns and rewards that get reinforced."

As she spoke, I was instantly transported back to sixth grade, Mr.

Moore's classroom, which he ran like a military unit, commanding respect without ever raising his voice. Mr. Moore was a straight shooter who gave praise sparingly. When he made it abundantly clear that I was head and shoulders above any other student, I felt *so* special. Mr. Moore took the time to answer my questions in a way that indicated to my eleven-year-old brain that he took me very seriously. While I felt like a pariah on the playground, when Mr. Moore held up my paper as an example to the others of the right way to do an assignment, I felt worthy.

But by high school, I was an addict, forever trying to re-create that first high I got in Mr. Moore's class. Avoiding the pain of awkward social interactions, I would spend lunchtime in the library studying for a test, and then literally glow with joy when I saw that A+ on my paper.

Neuroscientists might call this "synaptic pruning," which is a fancy term to describe a process your brain goes through when it prunes away less effective synaptic pathways, those neural routes that, for example, swiftly send a message from your brain that tells your hand to pull away from a hot stove. Synaptic pruning allows our brains to perform actions more efficiently—even behavioral actions that serve to protect us from hurt feelings as much as from burned fingers. Problem was, my young brain was exceedingly adept at avoiding pain and seeking pleasure—until I lost control of the process.

Just as an alcoholic cannot have a sip of wine without finding herself racing to the bottom of an endless bottle, there was never enough work, or money, or prestige, or accomplishments that would make me feel safe. I was addicted to *gettin' it done*, even though my obsession left me isolated, depleted, and utterly devoid of joy.

If you have lived with this struggle, Stanford professor and neuroscientist Dr. Andrew Huberman describes it in a way that may resonate: "Addiction is a progressive narrowing of the things that bring you pleasure. Enlightenment is an expansion of the things that bring you pleasure." I wonder, if workaholics could somehow tip the scales toward enlightenment, would we give up our to-do lists?

Before I spoke to Dr. Rebecca Heiss, I honestly thought that I had come to a clear understanding of what drove my workaholic's Never Enough mindset. But this conversation opened up a whole new biological piece of the puzzle for me. Hungry to learn more about the mechanisms of my work-obsessed brain, I called neuroscientist Dr. Marc Lewis.

In his beautifully written book, *The Biology of Desire*, Dr. Lewis tells us: "If we are to understand anything so complex and troubling as addiction, we need to gaze directly at the point where experience and biology meet. Because that's the bottleneck, the linchpin, where human affairs are cast and crystallized. That's where the brain shapes our lives and our lives shape the brain."

All of our experiences—from our small-*t* traumas, to the Counterfeit Financial Culture we engage in, and the workplace Hustle Culture that pushes us to do more—shape our brain, and vice versa. What I wanted to know from Dr. Lewis was this: What is happening in my brain when I'm telling myself, *I should turn off my computer, I really should sleep, I need to rest*—but instead, I rev the engines and race into an eighty-hour workweek that ends with me asleep in bed for two days?

"It's complicated, but I think that we could do a rough sketch of what's happening," Dr. Lewis said. As a neuroscientist, clinical psychologist, addiction expert, and someone who suffered from addiction in his twenties, he is candid about the fact that the physiological underpinnings of our behavior are often a mystery. Our highly complex nervous systems (the brain, spinal cord, and nerves) are constantly picking up real-time cues from our environment and then efficiently compelling us to think, move, and behave in certain self-protective ways in response. But when we are in the midst of a work binge, our brains often feel as if they are going rogue. That we are helpless to put on the brakes. In order to firmly take back control, it helps to know what is happening, biologically speaking, in the moments before we succumb to the binge.

"The pre-switch period, before you act, it's like you're pulling the reins on a horse," Dr. Lewis said. "And the lateral prefrontal cortex is in charge of that, it's in charge of inhibition."

As Dr. Lewis explained, the prefrontal cortex is the region of the brain involved in self-comprehension and self-regulation. The lateral part of your prefrontal cortex works to inhibit your behavior in different ways. For example, let's say your nervous system picks up a strong environmental cue, like a client who is visibly disappointed with something you said in a meeting. Her disapproval gnaws at you. Later, instead of going home at the end of your workday, you open up the client's project file, lose all track of time, forget to eat dinner, and toil until 2 a.m. The work addiction wins.

But let's take a closer look at this process. Because earlier, in the moments when your colleagues were shutting down their computers and heading out the door, that's when your lateral prefrontal cortex was trying to inhibit your predicted behavior (opening the project files and getting lost in them) *before* it happened.

"Meanwhile, the prefrontal cortex—the more executive, more thoughtful part—is trying like crazy to find other appraisals, other ways of framing things," Dr. Lewis continued.

So, where a heroin addict grappling with her own terrible pre-binge moment might pull on the reins by saying to herself, *I don't really need this drug. I don't like the way it makes me feel. I don't really want to do this*, a workaholic's prefrontal cortex will perform similar strategizing in an attempt to cut off the compulsive behavior: *I should really sleep on this problem. Working all night is only going to make me less productive tomorrow.* And just when your prefrontal cortex has almost convinced you to walk away from the compulsive behavior—cue the striatum.

The striatum is a region of the brain that's part of the limbic system, or our "motivational core," and it governs our impulsive and compulsive behaviors. As Dr. Lewis explains, "The striatum is in charge of behavior routines that are already well known, well-practiced, well-sequenced—all it really has to do is turn them on. And when dopamine comes up to the striatum . . . it turns on the striatum. When you're getting more and more dopamine coming from cues, it's that feeling of: *I've got to do something.*

I've got to do something. I've got to do something. That's when the striatum feels just too powerful and the balance tips between the striatum and the prefrontal cortex."

Far too many of us know that tipping point all too well. For example, when a compulsive binge-eater crosses over and begins to consume an entire pan of gooey brownies, a pint of salted-caramel ice cream, and tops it off with a gigantic piece of *tres leches* cake, it's because her well-meaning striatum won. Her striatum whispers: *Hush now, honey. Those painful feelings flooding your psyche? I know how to make that all go away . . . right now.* (I know this from firsthand experience.)

When I recall the countless work-binge tipping points of my past, I can almost hear my striatum murmuring to me: *Manisha, that client is so upset with you. Your boss is going to see how useless you are. Just let me handle it. I got this.* At that point I invariably allow my striatum to take the wheel and speed toward the nonstop *Doing* behaviors that I learned in grade school. By this point, the prefrontal cortex—the top-down part of our brains that inhibits harmful behaviors—has taken a backseat. And . . . we're off! Full speed ahead to the early-death-and-wrecked-relationships races.

Here's the million-dollar question that plagues all addicts—and I know it's like asking a climate scientist, "How do you solve global warming?" but I asked Dr. Lewis anyway: "So, from a brain perspective, when you're in that moment, the dopamine is flowing, and the striatum is like, 'I got this. Let go of the wheel, I got this,' how do you slow it down and avoid engaging in the addictive behavior?"

"Yeah," he said with a smile. "Well, that's *the* question, isn't it? I wish there was a simple answer." In other words, there is no one answer for everyone.

For many of the subjects in Dr. Lewis's book, the centuries-old practices of meditation and mindfulness have helped. My experience with meditation is that it really does give me a transitory sense of peace. Biologically speaking, it quiets my overactive striatum, giving control back to my executive-decision maker, the prefrontal cortex. (My problem is finding the discipline to do it in the moment my striatum starts screaming, not just for a few minutes at the start of each day.)

When I asked Dr. Lewis about any other tools that could help settle a workaholic's mind, he tells me that since he retired as a professor at the University of Toronto, a post he held for twenty-one years, he's come to almost exclusively see patients using a type of therapy called Internal Family Systems, or IFS.

The simplest way to describe IFS is that it honors all the different parts of your personality that guide your behaviors. It even names them, so you can begin a respectful dialogue with "the exiles," the child parts of your personality that experienced trauma; "the managers," who oversee, judge, and keep your exiles hidden; and "the firefighters," who swoop in with extreme and messy escapes, like, drug use, self-cutting, or working until you collapse.

Dr. Lewis was actually the third person with a PhD to ask me if I've tried IFS therapy. The first was workaholic expert Dr. Bryan Robinson, who uses it with his patients. The second: Dr. Rebecca Heiss.

"I will point you toward it, and you can revolt against it, Manisha. I won't be offended," she had said to me with her usual kindness. "But IFS therapy basically helps to address those little-t traumas. It allows you to just sit with that scared eleven-year-old, hear her, and tell her that she's safe. When we go back and visualize her being okay, not being rejected, it actually starts to heal and reroute those patterns of behavior so that we don't have to rally against them. We don't have to do these behaviors to prove ourselves."

In addition to IFS therapy, Dr. Heiss advocates taking slow baby steps toward behavioral change. For example, she suggests that workaholics practice drumming up dopamine release by setting small goals that do *not* involve work.

"Workaholics like a to-do list, right?" she says. "So write on your list: *Turn off computer at 7:50 p.m.* Then, when you achieve it—when you actually shut your computer off at 7:50 p.m.—you're going to get a *massive* hit of dopamine," she said, "because now, you're speaking the language that your brain recognizes: *I did it. I achieved my goal. I get the reward. I want more. I'm going to do it again tomorrow.*"

Another variation on this exercise, which involves embarrassing, scary, or new-to-you activities (what Dr. Heiss collectively refers to as "test-case stress"), gives the brain both a surge of dopamine *and* a dose of fear at the same time. For example, loudly singing a favorite song while driving your car to the grocery store or dancing alone in your living room can activate your nervous system's fight-or-flight response, even though these are relatively safe activities.

Dr. Heiss likes to quietly buy coffee for the person behind her in line at Starbucks, because it makes her feel really good (dopamine hit!) and it elicits stress. As you're standing in line, getting ready to tell the cashier what you'd like to do, your brain is reeling: *They're going to think you're so weird, they'll all laugh at you, don't do it!* You may barely feel the fear, but your brain does. And when you survive the moment, your brain discovers that not only did nobody reject you, but it felt great to make someone else's day.

From a biological perspective, what Dr. Heiss is telling us to do in order to rewire faulty neural patterns is to:

1. **Replicate the rewards** we get from unhealthy work behaviors (checking emails in bed) by setting easily achievable nonwork goals (turn computer off by 7:50 p.m.) that give us a similar dopamine hit. It also helps, she says, to write your goals down, as the act of writing creates a cognitive link, telling your brain: *This is the goal I want to achieve.*
2. **Unwind the fear** caused by little-*t* traumas by engaging in test-case stress—positive behaviors that feel scary at first (paying for coffee, singing loudly in your car, dancing alone to your favorite song,) but teach our brains that we can survive them.

Dr. Heiss gets excited talking about brain hacks. Her tempo quickened and I could almost see her smiling, even though we were on an old-fashioned phone call. Ever the dogged student, I was poised and taking notes as she was talking. But as a recovering workaholic, my cynicism kicked in *hard* when she brought up the practices she uses to achieve happier states—practices like visualization and gratitude journaling.

"This sounds too simplistic," I told her.

"Manisha, simple does *not* equate to easy," she said. "This stuff is actually *really* hard . . . because you have to get bored, take some breaths, sit with yourself—and that is one of the hardest things for your brain to do."

Hearing my resistance, she pointed me to the scientific evidence. One of her favorite studies comes from Harvard Medical School, where neuroscientists had nonmusician volunteers practice a five-finger piano exercise on an electric keyboard for two hours a day, five days a week, while the scientists studied the area of their brains that controlled motor movements. After five days of physical practice, the subjects all showed significant growth in the parts of their brains that were learning the new skill.

Next, they asked a new group of nonmusicians to do the same thing, but this time only using *mental* practice. These volunteers simply *imagined* themselves correctly playing the five-finger exercise. The results were stunning. Without ever touching a keyboard, the mental-practice group had the *same* brain changes as the participants who had physically practiced. In other words, merely *thinking* about a specific goal not only helped them to reach it, it actually rewired their brains to achieve it.

Apparently, mental practice is as routine as physical practice in the world of professional sports. Legendary golfer Tiger Woods says his father taught him to take a series of mental pictures of the swing he wanted to achieve, so that when he's in a tournament and feeling nervous, he tells himself, "C'mon, Tiger, just putt to the picture, just like Pop used to say." Five-time Olympian swimmer Michael Phelps not only imagined his perfect race, he also visualized all the things that could go wrong—a ripped suit, broken goggles—and then saw himself conquering these problems. In other words, he wired his brain to be prepared for anything that gets in the way of his goal.

Even the "soft" science of gratitude turns out to have hard evidence supporting it. When we feel grateful or give thanks to others, it actually activates neurochemical systems in the brain that release dopamine and serotonin, chemical messengers that enhance our moods and motivations. A groundbreaking 2003 study found that test subjects who kept a gratitude journal for ten weeks reported 25 percent happier moods than participants who were told to list things that annoyed them. Gratitude has also been found to help build resilience to post-traumatic stress disorder, improve sleep, enhance overall physical health, and the list goes on.

I felt my cynicism thawing when Dr. Heiss dove into the healing powers of spending time in nature. That is where I am *all in*. As a die-hard city girl, I recently discovered profound happiness after spending part of the summer at a small, one-room cabin on a lake in rural Maine.

"Yes, I *know* that nature works for me," I told her.

"That's fascinating," she said. "It's because you've experienced it."

That's it precisely: Our brains hew to what we believe to be true. If we believe that nature makes us feel alive and centered, then we will spend more time in nature. And if we believe that we're not good enough and that we have to achieve ever-greater heights to prove our worth, then our brains—and more specifically, our hardworking striatum—will dutifully follow.

"Let me ask you," Dr. Heiss said, "if you were to die tomorrow, what matters most? Does it matter that you got a bunch of compliments? Because I would argue that what you're really seeking *isn't* the compliment. And it's not the money or the prestige. Your brain is seeking the dopamine reward. So what would happen if you just walked away from work today, and walked toward the real things that make you happy?"

It didn't take me a second to reply: "That would be sheer bliss."

"So, what's stopping you?"

"The 'shoulds.' All the things I should be doing."

"Whenever I struggle from a case of the shoulds," she says, "I stop and ask, '*Who's* telling me I should? What is the cultural story or the little-*t* trauma that's saying, 'You *should* do this'? Because . . . maybe instead I should quit and walk away. Or maybe I decide to stay because *I* want to finish it."

My mind was instantly drawn to a project that was not working out. A project that was not a joyful or effective use of my time. Something I had been *told* I should do. Something I wanted to quit.

"So why don't you?" she asked. "Wouldn't it make you happier to put that time and energy into things you enjoy that *are* working?"

Just imagining letting that annoying project go, I could literally feel the muscles in my neck and shoulders release, my chest expand as my lungs joyfully filled with oxygen, and a smile starting to creep across my face. This was the biological evidence behind the brain-hacking visualization practice that Dr. Heiss speaks of.

"It never occurred to me to just give it up," I said.

"Runaway traits are like that," Dr. Heiss said. "All the things that we're doing are often to achieve the things that we already have. Our brains get that early wiring, and we end up chasing success to be happy, rather than being happy and then finding success."

o o o

The illuminating conversations I had with Drs. Heiss and Lewis simmered in my mind for the next few weeks as I put their wisdom into action. I watched a YouTube video about Internal Family Systems therapy. I meditated for five minutes. I gave myself a time-out from working on that project I hated (and *immediately* felt better!). I even started reading for pleasure in the mornings. Just fifteen minutes of my nose in a book before work, which felt like a small act of defiance, a positive cue, alerting my brain right at the start of the day that fun was allowed. It gave me something to look forward to before diving into my "shoulds."

As often happens when we're engaging in new disciplines, after a couple of weeks I started to slack off. For example, I would set a goal for the week of spending ten minutes outside walking on actual grass (not so easy in urban Portland). But then I wouldn't accomplish it. Or I'd skip a morning of reading if I had extra early meetings that day. Then I'd feel bad about myself for not completing my goals.

In other words, I had turned these helpful practices into assignments, another notation on my to-do list. And that's not the point, is it?

Reflecting on these experiences, I can see that I was trying to achieve everything all at once. But as Dr. Lewis reminds us, true healing from our addiction isn't likely to occur until we are "gazing directly at the point where experience and biology meet."

Everyone's process is unique. There is no single test or therapy protocol or brain hack that will fix our addictions and tame the Hungry Ghost. But *understanding* why we are hardwired to hustle gives us another arrow in our quivers to draw on when we are feeling unsafe.

For me, learning about what's happening in my brain and recognizing how my knee-jerk survival instincts were simply trying to protect me—it helped tremendously. I felt even more in control. It's not like a light switched on in my brain and suddenly I was cured. It's more like I was carrying a small candle in the dark: I can see that there's a path. I can sort of make out the way. It's dim, but there is light nonetheless.

Perhaps, in understanding the biological mechanisms of our problem in concert with all the other forces we've explored in this book, the wider body of knowledge creates a cumulative *knowing*. This deeper wisdom, or what Dr. Huberman calls "enlightenment," allows us to begin to transcend our primitive instincts and eventually take hold of the wheel.

Of course, relapse is normal and to be expected. I've had my own. Several times. Back when I was recovering from my bout with Epstein-Barr, I thought I had finally kicked my work addiction once and for all and was ready to re-embrace "simplicity" and "small joys." I returned to my job at the Seattle-based firm with excitement and a newfound sense that I was finally slowing down. But just a few weeks into my return I was forced to confront the real cost that I had paid for my toxic relationship with work and endless striving. It was a devastating discovery.

CHAPTER 6

Financial Health + Emotional Wealth = MoneyZen

"You're going to have to go out there and play this game called money. . . . But never forget that your friends and your family and your love of things that have nothing to do with money . . . those are your biggest treasures."

When I went back to work full-time in April 2020, my brain immediately snapped back into its old survival patterns, the same safety-seeking behaviors I had always relied on. But then something happened that made me feel completely exposed, like an addict at her own intervention.

It happened in mid-June 2020. I had a meeting scheduled with a prospective client, someone I had known for many years, who wanted to learn more about growing her money into retirement. It was a warm summer day and we gathered in a light-filled conference room. Sitting across from me were my colleagues, two female financial advisors from the firm. To my right sat my friend, a sixty-something successful artist, with perky, short brown hair and stylish red reading glasses.

Because she was a private person, and reluctant to lay her financial cards on the table, I decided to try something different that day: I would get financially naked, so to speak, by allowing the advisors to perform a real-time analysis of *my* finances. This way we could respect her privacy while demonstrating the power of what we could do for her.

Over the course of an hour, my colleagues walked me through my personal and professional history. I talked about my first real job, making minimum wage at seventeen, running the cash register and pumping gas for full-service customers at the Shell station back in Columbus, Indiana. I expressed how grateful I was that my parents were able (and wanted) to pay for all of my higher education. How, after graduating from college, I borrowed $2,000 from them to pay the first and last month's rent for a room in an apartment in New York that I shared with two girlfriends. I paid it all back within six months and never borrowed money from them again, I added, with no small amount of pride.

We traversed through three decades of career moves, investment decisions, and making a new home in Portland, Oregon, after my divorce. All the while, the advisors projected a running analysis of my finances on the screen. Based on my retirement goals, we looked at how much I could potentially spend per year if I never added another dollar to my investment accounts and what the odds would be, if I lived to different ages, of running out of money.

As the financial data points flashed up on the whiteboard in real time, it occurred to me that these numbers were not new to me—I'd done this analysis for myself. Many times, in fact. And yet, I'd never thought about these financial statistics in the context of my personal *life* story.

As we journeyed through the decades, I saw up close how my life had been driven by numbers. Or, more specifically, by reaching a single retirement number that would bring me a feeling of safety and security, or so I thought.

By the time we reached the present day, the fruits of my labors were plain to see: I was two months shy of turning fifty, and I could retire if I wanted. I had reached my goal. Tears began to stream down my face.

My friend turned to me and said, "You told me this process was powerful, but I didn't expect it to make you cry."

I had spent my entire life working toward this moment, toward a single magic number. Getting here was no small feat, and I knew that I should have been celebrating. But as I apologized and wiped away my tears so we could get back to my friend and *her* financial needs, I could feel myself slowly sinking into an existential crisis.

As the advisors resumed their presentation, turning to interest rates, trusts, and living wills, I felt a wave of nausea roll through me. Seeing those numbers on the whiteboard—it was the first time I really felt in my core that I was financially safe. Yet the price for that security had been exorbitant. It had quite literally cost me my life. To put it another way, I was a model of financial health, but I had no emotional wealth to speak of.

This realization felt like a hard slap to the face. How many life-affirming experiences had I left on the table in the pursuit of ever more work, money, and prestige? And how was I going to get that time *back*?

The truth, I knew, was that I wasn't. Just shy of my fiftieth birthday, most likely over half my life was gone, and I had nothing to show for it except the privilege of a potential early retirement—a scenario that filled me with dread, because if I stopped working now that would mean I could no longer hide behind my work. I'd have to figure out how to finally start living. It was all I ever wanted. It was everything I feared.

o o o

There are myriad reasons why we get caught up in the hamster wheel of Never Enough. As we saw in Chapter 5, even our own biology can drag us around that racetrack. But now that we've examined the many factors that can result in a toxic relationship with money, work, and achievements, in Chapters 6 and 7 I want to switch gears and start examining the elements of a new mindset, one that warmly embraces that what we have and who we are is *Enough*.

In my case, it was impossible to achieve this mindset until I gave up an insidious belief I'd long internalized: **self-worth = net worth**.

Convinced that the more money I made, the more worthy I was as a human being, I had optimized my life around this equation. I believed that once I hit my magic retirement number, I'd finally feel safe and powerful, and no one could ever hurt me again. Of course, writing that down, I can see the absurdity of such a belief. No amount of money can shield any of us from life's inevitable pains.

"If you struggle with 'enough,' more money won't solve that problem. It's the wrong tool for the job," my friend Carl Richards once told me. "That's because 'enough' is not a money problem, it's an emotional problem. It's a fulfillment problem. It's a problem for therapy. We've given money a job that it was not intended to do."

When I told Richards about my own experience at forty-nine, finally reaching that magic retirement number that was going to give me peace of mind and a guarantee that I finally had *enough*, he smiled and asked, "And has it worked?"

"No."

"That's because 'enough' is a different kind of problem. It's a problem of loneliness, it's a problem of connection, it's a problem of abandonment. These are deeper problems."

He's right. Making us feel whole is not money's job. Don't get me wrong. I'm not saying—and Richards is definitely not saying—that money isn't important or that all you need is love. Financial stability is, inarguably, essential to one's health and well-being. But as someone who has spent a lifetime honing her moneymaking prowess at the tragic expense of her relationships and health, I can say with authority that financial wealth alone does not render a portrait of a well-lived life.

Money alone cannot get us to the place where we feel safe or that we are enough. Money is like a car with no gas. It's good to have, but without the emotional fuel of curiosity, connection, and creative pursuits—where are you gonna go?

Here's what I know now, with deep certainty: Emotional wealth is equally as important—if not *more* important—as financial wealth.

In fact, I would argue that it's time we completely flipped the narrative about the role money plays in our lives. Let's stop covering up our small-*t* traumas with Busy Badges. Let's resist the unsustainable demands of Counterfeit Financial Culture. Let's refuse to bow to the pressures of Hustle Culture. Let's take back control of our biology and redirect our primitive impulses to helping rather than harming us. All of these factors led me to strive for the unreachable equation of net worth = self-worth—and they likely have led you to some unrealistic ideas about the role of money in your own life, too.

So what if we adopted a whole new way to think about work, money, achievements, and praise? What if instead of living to optimize an equation (self-worth = net worth) that by its very nature has no end, and leaves us forever striving for more, more, *more*—what if we aimed for a new equation:

Financial Health + Emotional Wealth = MoneyZen

Put another way, if we stopped chasing after "financial wealth" and set a more reasonable goal of financial health, we could free up the time, space, and energy to begin accumulating a deeper, more meaningful stockpile of emotional wealth. We could finally reach our own level of MoneyZen.

What do these concepts actually mean? We'll focus on financial health + emotional wealth in this chapter and MoneyZen in the next. But for now, think of MoneyZen as the antidote to Never Enough. It's a mentality in which you are able to operate on a day-to-day basis with calm, confidence, and clarity around your work and finances because you are clear about the role money plays in your life and you innately know how to use it wisely, and in ways that make your heart sing. In the pages ahead, I'll explore **financial health** and **emotional wealth** one at a time, so you can think about these ideas in relation to your own financial circumstances and emotional needs.

To be clear, this book is not a primer on personal finance. I'm not going to tell you what kind of insurance to buy, or why to have a pre-nuptial agreement, or how to pay for college. I've already cowritten two personal finance books focused on helping people to get their accounts in order, and there are plenty more excellent books and online resources, with information for virtually every stage of life and financial dilemma. (See my website MoneyZen.com for a curated list of resources, broken out by financial topic.)

As I mentioned in Chapter 1, money worries are distinct from money *problems.* In countries like the United States, where we have few or thin social safety nets to protect us in the face of unexpected health crises, job losses, or suddenly having to become a full-time caregiver—financial health is not guaranteed for everyone. There are larger policy issues at play for which a change in mindset alone is not going to solve these kinds of terrible money problems.

However, if you're making enough money to be mostly debt-free and to care for your loved ones—what was called a "competence" back in the day, as we learned in Chapter 3—then you've already achieved what many might call financial health. For some, that feels like a gift. For others, it still looks like not enough. There is no single portrait of financial health that suits everyone. But what I've found for myself, and for the clients and students I work with who represent a wide spectrum of income levels, is that it's impossible to determine what "enough" is if we are not crystal clear about the job that money performs in our lives.

In other words, we can't reach Money Zen until we identify the proper balance of "financial health" and "emotional wealth" that works in our own, unique lives. So let's take a closer look at how to reach MoneyZen by better balancing two goals: financial health *and* emotional wealth.

FINANCIAL HEALTH

To put it simply: Financial health is when your books are balanced (for example, you meet your regular monthly expenses and pay at least your minimum monthly debt payments on time) and you still have some money left over to cover an emergency and to set aside funds for the future. As we learned in earlier chapters, that's no easy task given that we are surrounded by societal messaging that implores us to buy, buy, buy (*the latest iPhone, a table at the trendy new nightclub, the most expensive sunglasses*). Ironically, at the same time, financial fads shame us for spending *any* money at all. Financial health is not about racing to retire by age fifty, although that might happen. Financial health is about having *enough* (more about defining your enough in Chapter 7).

In my thirty years of helping people manage their money, I've seen firsthand how easy it is to get caught up in obsessive trends that tell us we do not have nearly enough and so we must starve ourselves of life's pleasures now in order to enjoy what remains of our life later. Just as Hustle Culture can push us to exhaustion and burnout, there are powerful financial narratives around saving money that fuel harmful, life-draining behaviors.

One of the most popular examples of this, an approach I've followed myself at various points in my life, is FIRE, or Financial Independence/Retire Early. The goal of FIRE is to achieve a "work-optional" life by saving 50 to 70 percent of your annual income (yes, *50 to 70 percent!*) until you've amassed your "FIRE number." There are different ways to calculate your FIRE number but, essentially, you determine your annual expenses, then multiply that number by 25 to discover the amount of money you have to save in order to Retire Early. If that sounds like an impossible figure to achieve in a lifetime, *that's* the math underlying such draconian savings rates.

Today there are a multitude of blogs, books, YouTube channels, and conferences in which FIRE enthusiasts passionately preach their aggressive cost-cutting practices. This runaway movement was originally inspired by *Your Money or Your Life*, a book first published in 1992 by my dear friend Vicki Robin and her late coauthor, Joe Dominguez. The goal of their book, which has sold over a million copies and is in its fourth edition, was to teach us how to live a meaningful life that honors earth and community. The goal was *not* to become a multimillionaire by forty. Their intention was to encourage us to spend mindfully and in accordance with our values. This is what financial health looks like. But some readers took their mindful-spending advice as a directive to deny themselves everything from an $8 craft beer in a brewery with friends to a $15-an-hour babysitter who could have allowed a tired couple some much-needed alone time.

"I was so surprised to encounter the FIRE movement," Robin recently told me. Curious to learn more about the community, she attended FIRE retreats, where experts gave speeches and consulted with new adherents. She found that few followers seemed to share her values.

"Nice people. Especially the bloggers—sassy, smart, kind, just pouring out their knowledge to help others and build their brands. But I was disappointed," she said. "Our goal was environmental, to take the pressure off the natural systems of the planet and to wake people up from the consumer game."

Robin said she spent a couple of years trying to "level-up the intentions of the FIRE movement . . . to encourage a social conscience." But from what I can tell, many of us turned her book's sustainability lessons into a competition: Spend even *less*, and reach a *bigger* retirement nest egg, *faster!*

Here's the key flaw in that game, a lesson I learned too late: What's the point in becoming a millionaire by forty if you've not spent a dollar on *living your life?*

That was exactly what Ani, the thirty-five-year-old yoga teacher we met in Chapter 1, struggled with when her family embarked on their own FIRE quest several years ago. They had always been a frugal couple, with a sound base of financial health and emotional wealth. But with a growing family, and student loans to pay back, they embarked on a FIRE lifestyle that quickly got competitive and intense.

"We started doing it when my husband was in law school," Ani told me. "At first, he wanted to do it for as short a time as possible. But then he got *really* into it. Soon it was like we could never be frugal enough—he was obsessed with FIRE." Every expenditure was agonized over, even at the grocery store, where Ani would push to buy the better-tasting organic tomatoes while her husband argued that the cheaper ones would suffice.

"To be fair," she said, "we are extremely privileged people, so *our* frugal would be somebody else's luxurious. But we were just not enjoying life because we weren't doing anything. We were only trying to save, save, save and pay off student loan debt."

In other words, they put all their eggs in the financial wealth basket, leaving them void of emotional wealth. But then, Ani said, at a certain point, her husband had a literal "come to Jesus" moment.

"He was so unhappy, and hated his job, and he started going to church. That's when he realized he wasn't living," she said. "He was like, 'Jesus would not be hoarding money. I want to be easygoing about money. I want to be more generous, and forgiving, and compassionate, and have more fun.'"

Soon they were paying a babysitter so they could go out, just the two of them, once a week. They loosened the reins when it came to price versus quality, knowing that sometimes the more expensive choice lasts longer or brings you more pleasure.

It's not that they turned their back on FIRE, or started giving their money away in buckets. It's that they got back to a better balance of financial health + emotional wealth. Rather than engaging in all-or-nothing financial decision-making—and suffering and feeling resentful about purchases—they became more intentional about money. They spent it in ways that nourished their souls and brought them closer as a couple and as a family.

"FIRE was pretty good for us because now we don't have much debt hanging over our heads and we're on a good path to retirement," Ani said. "But there was a period where it caused a lot of tension in our marriage. Now we'll get the organic tomatoes because they taste better, but we'll be reasonable about apples—I'll be like, 'Okay, they taste the same, so let's just get the regular apples.'"

Once they changed their perspective on the job of money, they were able to use it in ways that allowed them "to be more generous, and forgiving, and compassionate, and have more fun," just as they'd dreamed. By rebalancing the scales of financial health and emotional wealth, they achieved their own level of MoneyZen.

"My husband was kind of struggling with money before," Ani said, "but he has become such a better person. I have mad respect for him."

There's nothing wrong with encouraging people to save money, spend wisely, and build a retirement fund. That's an empowering financial routine that I wish more people were able to do on a consistent basis. Rather, it's the extreme frugality being paraded on blogs, YouTube videos, and subreddit posts that give me pause.

When I asked Carl Richards to weigh in on FIRE, he likened it to fad dieting: "There's immediate rewards, and you see results . . . but the dilemma is, again, it's just placing the focus on the wrong thing. FIRE is not going to lead to happiness."

When movements like FIRE are practiced competitively, obsessively— they become another entry point to the Cult of Never Enough. It's a healthy goal taken to a harmful extreme.

So instead of seeing money as something we need to collect and hoard—or, alternately, as an instrument of control that's shameful and should be avoided entirely—what if instead we saw money as a tool that allows us to chase greater emotional wealth? Instead of spending our precious years trying to add more zeroes to our bank balances, what if we build a base of financial health that gives us the flexibility to put more of what truly lights us up into our lives. What if we aimed for having a calm and *conscious* experience around spending?

As Vicki Robin explained it, working ceaselessly to reach a specific number was never her goal. Rugged financial individualism does not interest her. The *common good* has always been her endgame. To that end, she personally invests in her own community, provides low-interest loans to local entrepreneurs who share her environmental values, and has even arranged for her home to be donated to a local sustainability nonprofit, giving them the freedom to determine the greatest need for its use after she's gone.

Robin's MoneyZen mindset is uniquely attuned to her personal values. She is very clear about the role money plays in her life and how to use it to create more connection, community, and common good—all of which generate wonderful opportunities for her to achieve greater emotional wealth.

When I ask Robin what she would tell the next generation about how to use money rather than be used by it, she reminds us, "Individualism is one of the biggest bamboozles of the consumer culture . . . remember, you're going to have to go out there and play this game called money. You're going to get an education, you're going to be clever, you're going to figure it out. But never forget that your friends and your family and your love of things that have nothing to do with money—whether it's nature or hobbies or whatever—*those* are the things that are most important. Those are your biggest treasures."

Her wisdom is worth repeating: *Your friends and family and your love of things that have nothing to do with money are your biggest treasures.* Let's dig deeper into what those things might be.

EMOTIONAL WEALTH

Emotional wealth is about living a full, intentional life. There is no one portrait of emotional wealth that suits everyone. For me, I know I'm experiencing it when I want to get out of bed as soon as the alarm goes off. It's a feeling that the day is about to open up like a flower—and I can't wait to see what it looks like. It's about lingering, exploring, and discovering all the small moments and experiences that bring me joy.

On the flip side, I know that I *don't* have emotional wealth when I keep pulling the covers over my head and hitting the snooze button. Or when I get that Sunday-dread feeling because I worked all weekend, Monday is on my heels, and I'm going to have to start the next wind sprint.

Like anything worthwhile, seeking greater emotional wealth requires practice. So how does one start? It may help to begin with a few probing questions that can illuminate your unique path to a life well lived. For example:

- When in my life was I the happiest? Where was I? What was I doing?
- What one step can I take toward happiness *right now*?
- What creative activities did I once do that brought me joy?
- Where would I live if I could be anywhere in the world?
- Who are the people in my life who most *get* me and I want to reconnect with?
- What are three places on earth I want to explore before I die?
- If I could change one thing about my relationships with my parents, siblings, partner, children, or other relatives, what would it be?
- If I could spend a week with my closest friends, where would we go and what would we do?

One question I've posed to clients and audiences from an extremely wide range of incomes at workshops over the years is this: If you won $10 million in the lottery and, on the same day, were told you had only ten years left to live, what would you *start* doing and what would you *stop*? The purpose of this exercise is to consider what changes you would make in your life if you no longer had any financial constraints but you had a very stark time constraint. How would you spend your time?

These questions are meant to help you better balance your own scales of financial health + emotional wealth, so you can move toward Money-Zen in a way that is personal to your life's values. In answering them, you'll soon begin to rediscover the different *realms* or *concepts* in your life that bring you the greatest joy. Perhaps spending time with family makes you really happy. For others, it might be exercise, nature, travel, or learning a new skill. And of course, these can change, expand, or narrow as you continue to explore what gives you pleasure.

Let me expand on this concept, by sharing my own experiences with this exercise. For example, when I ask these questions of myself, I can pinpoint three concepts that help to create greater emotional wealth in my own life. They are: **Connection**, **Creativity**, and **Authenticity**. I'll elaborate on each of these below, but remember: What makes your heart sing will be totally unique to you!

Emotional Wealth via Connection

As the world went into lockdown during the Covid pandemic, social scientists everywhere stressed that we remain socially connected even as we socially distance. That's because human connection is central to our mental and physical health, according to nearly a century of scientific research. In fact, I want to give Connection the biggest spotlight in this section, because it's often a straight path toward greater emotional wealth.

Studies find that loneliness (which is the opposite of human connection) is as risky to our health as smoking, obesity, and high blood pressure. Researchers at the University of California, Los Angeles, recently discovered that being lonely causes a molecular-level impact on our bodies, increasing the kind of inflammation that can cause cancer, Alzheimer's, and other chronic conditions, while decreasing our body's ability to mount a proper immune response to these diseases.

On the flip side, strong social connections act as a protective measure on our health, helping to speed our recovery from major illness and even increase our life spans. The renowned Harvard Study of Adult Development, which began in 1938, tracked 724 men (the second-generation study will involve women), asking the subjects and their families detailed questions, every two years, about their happiness and well-being, while also collecting biological samples and raw physical data. What the researchers found is that genetics alone does not promise a good life. The men who report satisfying relationships with family, friends, and community also tend to lead longer, more fulfilling lives, with less physical and cognitive decline.

What does all this togetherness have to do with beating back a Never Enough mindset? It seems that regular social connection may help to stave off harmful, compulsive behaviors. In a fascinating series of experiments from the late 1970s, which have come to be known as the Rat Park studies, Canadian psychologist Bruce Alexander and his team at Simon Fraser University found that when a rat is put in a cage alone and given a choice of plain water or water laced with morphine, it will choose morphine until it drinks itself to death. But when Alexander placed the animals in a rat colony, filled with engaging toys and lots of rat friends, they were much less likely to choose the toxic water. They played, mated, and raised babies. In other words, if kept alone, rats will self-medicate themselves to death; but social connection and a stimulating environment protected the animals against their own self-destructive behaviors.

Returning to humans, Dr. Belinda Campos, a psychological scientist who is a professor and chair of the department of Chicano/Latino Studies at the University of California, Irvine, has found in her research that Latinos tend to report higher levels of happiness than non-Latinos, even in the face of fewer economic resources. Intrigued, I called Dr. Campos to pick her brain about this money-happiness paradox.

Campos, who is Latina, explains that while rugged individualism is common in American and some European cultures, the first- and second-generation U.S.-based Latinos in her studies tend to retain a strong belief that family needs outweigh individual desires. Even the word *obligation*, which sounds like a heavy burden in English, has a more positive connotation in Spanish. *Obligación* means you're always there for the people who need you.

"We get joy out of work," she tells me. "But we do not make work our entire life. Our lives revolve around our relationships, our family, our neighborhoods, our social organizations. And I'm going to argue to you that it's probably the key to that paradoxical finding that people across Latin America tend to be happier than we would think, given the income levels of the countries."

Dr. Campos points to an American military study from 1982 that found that it was harder to retain Hispanic recruits because they felt that they could ask for leave to attend the bedside of a sick parent or the funeral of an immediate family member, but they were penalized for requesting leave for happier events, such as the baptisms or *quinceañeras* of second- and third-degree relatives—even though these milestones were equally as important to the recruits.

Honestly, this shocked me when I first heard it: Take time off for a happy event? No doubt it's an important moment, but the idea of missing work to attend, say, a cousin's bat mitzvah was so foreign to my brain, it's like asking me if I would go to the office in my underwear. But Campos tells me that when you are socialized to believe that this is a normal and expected part of your life, you tend to report greater levels of happiness than those who live independent, self-oriented lives.

In Latino countries, she says, *"trabajar para vivir."* You work to live. But in the United States, it's *"vivir para trabajar."* You live to work.

Humbled, I'm reminded of the time in my marriage when I got so angry at my ex-husband for telling someone that we didn't live to work, we worked to live. *What a dumb thing to say,* I thought at the time, naively.

Today I have a new approach. I've built deeper connections to my partner, Jay; my entire family; and my community at large. For example, Jay makes it so easy for us to connect as a couple. Every morning, when the alarm goes off, he brings two steaming cups of coffee into the room, crawls back into bed, and we just talk and laugh, snuggling up in the cozy flannel sheets for the next half hour or so. It's my favorite time. No matter what happens next, my day has kicked off with a delightful dose of emotional wealth.

Our routine even colors my connection to my community, as I move through my day with a greater outward (rather than inward) focus. For example, I love it when family, friends, and colleagues ask me to speak to their teenage or young adult sons and daughters about the basics of handling their money. Often, I start one of these conversations thinking, *Okay, I'll keep this to twenty minutes . . .* and next thing I know, not only have we talked for an hour, but I'm truly excited for this young person to reconnect with questions for me as their lives unfold. The innate joy I get from helping and supporting them is enough to make time stop and that joyous flow state kick in.

Family connection is everything to me now. Since my parents are in their eighties, I've started FaceTiming them for a few minutes, every day of the week if I can. We share mundane highlights from our days, thoughts on world events, news from extended family. I always, *always*, step away from those calls with a smile.

Additionally, some of my biggest emotional wealth deposits come when I'm connecting with my brother's kids. Recently, during a work trip in Los Angeles, I was rushing to get to a carnitas bowl at one of my favorite small eateries before it closed at 5 p.m.; just as I arrived, my phone rang. It was my eight-year-old nephew, FaceTiming me from the East Coast before his bedtime.

"Hi, sweetie," I said. "I can't talk now; I need to get some food and the place is about to close."

"Mishi," he said in a stern voice, "you can eat anytime, but I may not always want to talk to you."

He was right. In fact, he had saved up the entirety of his daily allotted screen time just to speak with me. So, I sat down, cross-legged, on the curb to chat with him about his latest passions: custom-building Lego structures and all things Harry Potter. We talked and talked. And while my stomach might have been growling, my soul was nourished. I felt true peace because connection builds emotional wealth like nothing else.

Emotional Wealth via Creativity

Although I once would have rolled my eyes at the notion, opening up space in your life for creativity is not a woo-woo idea. Scientific data show that creative endeavors can enhance your immune system, stave off dementia, improve your mood, and even help to create novel neural patterns as your brain struggles to learn a new skill. Engaging in creative acts lights up the reward centers of our brains in ways that are longer lasting and more sustainable than the rewards we get from being busy. In this way, creativity is a powerful antidote to harmful Hustle Culture.

Some people exercise their artistic muscles by painting, drawing, singing, gardening, journaling, dancing, or engaging in performing arts. For me, I like to reach back to the things that have always brought me joy: music, language, and travel.

As many adults will tell you, I so regret that I gave up on piano in high school (you were *right*, Mom!). Determined to wake up my brain's music muscles, I recently acquired a used Roland digital countertop keyboard and found two nifty piano apps (Simply Piano and Flowkey) that serve as my digital piano teachers. On any given day, when I feel like I need a break from work, I love sitting in front of the keyboard, warming up with my beginner scales, and practicing a few more bars of the latest piece of Baroque music (the easy version!) that I'm learning.

I'm also brushing up on my Spanish using the Duolingo app. My passion for all things *Español* began when I spent one summer in high school studying Spanish in San Luis Potosí, a gorgeous city in central Mexico, where I strictly followed the rules of not uttering a single word of English during the entire ten-week program. Later, when I lived in Texas and in New Mexico, I felt a deep sense of connection and camaraderie when speaking Spanish with anyone who let me practice with them.

As for my travel pursuits, I'm finally in a head space where I *want* to take vacations—and truly unplug—because I recognize how important travel is for my mental and physical health. Traveling with Jay, we get to connect more deeply as we explore far-flung locales that we've always wanted to see and take on adventures that speak to our shared interests. And whenever a work trip brings me nearer to my parents' or my brother's homes, I make a point of tacking on a few extra days to spend time with them.

EMOTIONAL WEALTH VIA AUTHENTICITY

This last realm is fairly simple in concept: *How am I being in the world? And how do I want to be?* In other words, if I'm pulling back from being a doer—if work no longer defines me—then what *is* my authentic self?

For those of us who struggle with a sense of identity when we are not working, this is a crucial question to reflect on. We have to give ourselves permission to connect with others in a way that does not involve competition. We have to engage in the kind of self-talk that reminds us: *You have nothing to prove. You don't need to parade your bonus numbers, your four-digit handbags, or any other self-worth anchors to anyone in order to measure up here. You have permission to just be you.*

When you act authentically, the wonderful part is that you allow everyone around you to be *their* authentic selves, too. You'll make stronger connections, which will inspire you to be more creative. And as you allow that creativity to flow, even more of your real, authentic self emerges. It's a beautiful, virtuous cycle.

For example, this morning I went to my favorite coffeehouse wearing stretchy black pants, a red-and-black woodsman's flannel shirt, comfortable slip-on shoes, my hair up in a clip, no makeup, and my beige heavy-duty canvas backpack slung over my shoulders. (Even at the age of fifty-two, I sometimes dress like a college student; perhaps because it reminds me of that wonderful feeling that your whole life is ahead of you, like a blank canvas.) I spent several hours writing, with the sun streaming in through the windows, classical music in my ears. It felt *so* good to not be tethered to a four-digit bag or killer-CEO spiked heels. That armor is no longer authentic to who I am, or who I want to *be*.

o o o

What does emotional wealth look like for you? When and where do you find authentic joy? The answers are different for everyone. I recently asked my MoneyZen newsletter subscribers to tell me about the ways that they find emotional wealth. Their responses were so good, I'm sharing a small handful here in case they inspire you to think more deeply about how to stock up your own happy reserves.

Q. Where do you find emotional wealth?
- Reading a good, inspiring, spiritual book; working out in a gym/swimming; taking a nature walk with lush-leafy vegetation.
- My family (including the dog), connection to friends and yoga students, and my yoga and meditation practice.
- The mountains, my artistic practice—watercolor painting and ceramics.
- Meditation, twelve-step recovery friends, gratitude practice.
- Enjoying a life with my amazing daughter after struggling so hard to have her; the support of a tight neighbor community that feels like family.

Connection, Creativity, and Authenticity are touchstones I reach out to as often as possible to enhance my emotional wealth—and to stay true to my new life-affirming equation:

Financial Health + Emotional Wealth = MoneyZen

But with anything worthwhile, choosing emotional wealth over the relentless pursuit of work, money, and prestige takes *practice.* It requires shifting our black-and-white perspectives and rewiring old neural patterns. I liken it to flipping a light switch on or off.

For example, my brain used to be constantly stuck in the *ON* position, toiling over "real" work, while shutting out the things that brought me joy, until when it was time to crash, burn, and sleep it *OFF.* But now I can see clearly that there isn't just *one* on-or-off switch in my toolkit. There's a wide variety of dimmer switches, labeled "yoga," "reading," "Jay time," "nature," "piano," and more. And, yes, I have several for "work," too.

Tomorrow, I might turn up the "research" dimmer to do some meeting prep for a mutual fund board I sit on. Other days, I'll crank up the nature knob by journaling in a hammock and then going for a swim or kayak in a nearby lake. As a former on-or-off type of person, it's such a relief to see that I have choices and they exist on a wide spectrum.

You do, too. You can turn your dimmers up or down slowly to reach whatever level of intensity or chillness that you want. For instance, instead of calendaring one hour a day of Spanish, five days a week, into my agenda—and then feeling bad when I can't possibly achieve that goal— I'll spend five minutes on my Duolingo app and then ten minutes on Simply Piano when the mood hits. And it hits surprisingly often.

For years, I treated Saturday and Sunday as bonus workdays, opportunities to get ahead. Many of us do this. We take every opportunity to focus on improving our financial wealth at the expense of our flagging emotional wealth. But as I write this, I'm about to embark on my third weekend in a row of not working—which feels *really* good. Using weekends to rest is a gift. Taking those two days to recharge gives us so much more insight and clarity about what's important in life. Likewise, taking intraday breaks between projects to read a chapter of a novel or just sit outside and appreciate the fresh air—these are small joys we often feel there's never enough time in the day to do, but they are crucial to our health and well-being.

Of course, there will be weeks when I have several time-sensitive projects to finish, so the work dimmer temporarily goes up to 9, and yoga goes down to 0. If you find yourself slipping on occasion, don't beat yourself up over it. Not every day will be a symphony. As workaholics, we often believe that we have to do every single thing perfectly and intensely. But we really don't. Perfection is not only unhealthy and unreasonable, but unattainable. Instead we can aim for incremental progress. We can achieve less, and it's okay.

Looking back, that fateful June 2020 financial planning meeting with my prospective client turned into a heartbreaking and lifesaving wake-up call. I left work that day feeling an odd mix of raw sadness and nascent hope. It had never been clearer that my flawed self-worth = net worth mindset had taken a high toll. Yet I also felt a sense of hope and excitement. For the first time in my adult life, I realized I didn't have to keep running. I could just be.

By June 30, 2020, I said good-bye to the truly wonderful company I worked for, with a stream of apologies, a gnawing sense of fear over my future, and immense guilt over leaving one of the best jobs I've ever had.

But crossing to the other side of fifty in just a couple of months was far scarier. The very idea left me with a desperate desire to catch up on all the living that I'd left on the table. It was finally time to flip the balance of my life's energy. But to do that, I had to go discover what "enough" looked like.

CHAPTER 7

———

The Liberation of Enough

Subtract to find your enough, and it will give you the time
and space to discover what really matters to you.

I once heard a heartbreaking tale about how elephants in captivity are trained. It's a story of learned helplessness that goes like this:

In the wild, elephants are nomads. They can roam for miles a day, grazing, swimming, socializing, and wandering with their herd. They are highly social animals. But this is not the case for working elephants in captivity.

When a baby elephant reaches a certain age, the trainer will chain one or more of its legs to a metal post in the ground. The frightened and frustrated young pachyderm will cry, tug, and fight to the point of exhaustion to free itself. But it simply does not have the strength to rip out the anchor that grounds it.

After many months of this routine, the animal simply gives up and accepts her tight confines. At some point, the trainer takes off the chain and replaces it with a rope, or even a flimsy piece of string. It doesn't matter that this tether is no match for the elephant's sheer strength and would be easy for her to break free from. She no longer tries to leave the area in which she is kept. Her mind is a prison: *I cannot leave. I will not leave. What's the point of trying to explore beyond this enclosure?*

This story resonates with a lot of Never Enough cult members I know who have come to accept their circumstances as inflexible facts. We get so accustomed to our constricting ideas about work, money, and prestige that we don't even consider what life might be like beyond our self-imposed prisons. We believe the financial funhouse mirrors that trick us into thinking everyone else has more—and we should, too. We accept narratives around do-it-all Hustle Culture that do not reflect reality. And, tragically, we aren't even aware that we have the power to release ourselves from the imaginary boundaries of a Never Enough mindset.

But just imagine, for a moment, what it might be like to roam the wide terrain of life—to seek greater social connections, spend time in nature, find your creative gifts, and explore all the things that bring you greater emotional wealth. How would it feel to silence the voice in your head that constantly orders you to *be* more, *do* more, *have* more? If you could escape the confines of the Never Enough mindset for a day and roam free with no repercussions, where would you go? What would you do?

I often picture the Never Enough mindset as an invisible chain, one that keeps us tethered to the parts of our lives that don't serve us, that are making us sick and miserable. With that in mind, I would encourage you to consider this question: What is your invisible chain? What's stopping you from breaking it? Maybe it's a magic retirement number that only ever increases. Or perhaps it's a belief that you must prove yourself worthy in the eyes of society to compensate for past traumas that made you feel undeserving or unsafe. Who or what is telling you that you should do more? How would it feel to turn the volume on those voices down and explore the wide world of connection and joy that awaits you just beyond the four corners of your desk?

In the previous chapter we examined what a life driven by the equation of financial health + emotional wealth = MoneyZen might look like for you as an individual. We saw how emotional wealth comes from the things that bring you joy—perhaps reading a book, taking a sunrise hike, volunteering at a women's shelter, or exploring a new city. We also determined that true financial health isn't about severe deprivation or vast wealth. Financial health represents what you require to meet your baseline economic needs and for you to feel comfortable; it's that place where you know you have *enough*.

In this chapter, I want to show you how to escape the cold and sterile confines of Never Enough so you can begin to envision a new way of life. We'll consider the stories of people I've met on this journey who have successfully kept emotional wealth and financial health front of mind when seeking their own liberation. I'll share a few practical tools that have helped me, and which I very much hope can help you, to stay on the path toward financial health + emotional wealth. And you will begin to redefine what "enough" means to you, personally.

Therein lies the rub for most of us: What the heck does "enough" look like? How will you know when you've reached enough financial health? And what does enough emotional wealth feel like? These are the questions I recently posed to Carl Richards, whom we first met in Chapter 3 and heard from again in the last chapter.

"The challenge with *enough*," he said, "is that there's no formula for it. My own definition of enough is: I know it when I feel it, and I also know when I'm out of enoughness—and it has very little to do with money."

Money was once my sole measure of enoughness. But seeing the numbers in my bank account go up didn't make me feel whole, because that's not the job money is meant to do. But if money is not what paves the way on the road to "enough," then what *is* its essential role in our lives?

"To me, it's freedom. What else?" says my very smart friend Helaine Olen, a *Washington Post* columnist and coauthor of the critically acclaimed book *The Index Card*. "And people define freedom in different ways: freedom to walk out of a job, freedom to move across the country, freedom to buy the down quilt you really like, freedom to take their dog to the vet."

The baby elephant story tells us that freedom is often a state of mind. And as Olen points out, money is a powerful tool that can help us to activate a sense of liberation. But Never Enough cult members like me tend to turn money (and its bedfellows prestige and accomplishments) into an addiction, a competition, or a crutch. Instead of being an agent of freedom, money becomes a prison.

That was certainly my experience. I used money to fortify the walls that kept me isolated from actually living my life. I believed that money created an impenetrable shield of safety around me, so that I would never feel stuck, wounded, or rejected. But that shield was a mirage, akin to that flimsy bit of rope around the baby elephant's foot.

Today, however, money is no longer a protective wall to me. It's a tool to explore what brings me joy. This means I will fly to Washington, D.C., for my nephews' and niece's birthdays, even when ticket prices are high, because it's more important to be with family than to hold on to that money. Or I will choose to spend an entire afternoon sitting by a lake, reading an engrossing book, and not worry about the fact that I'm not earning money during that time.

Richards recently told me a story that perfectly encapsulates the difference between a MoneyZen "I have enough" mindset and a money-first "Never Enough" mindset. It began when one of his four kids called him to say, "Dad, I want to spend my spring break with you."

"When your twenty-three-year-old daughter tells you that she wants to spend spring break with *you*, you say 'yes,'" he said with a parent's knowing laugh. "So we went to Baja, Mexico, and surfed. It was amazing. Totally by ourselves, no one else in the water, no one on the shore, we sat around the fire every night."

For four days, Richards and his daughter bonded in nature during a time of year when most twenty-somethings her age are partying with their classmates. It was a meaningful trip that they'll always remember. But upon his return home, a very wealthy friend told Richards that his behavior was incredibly irresponsible, upbraiding him with admonitions along the lines of *Why would you take off so much time from work? You should be focusing on building intergenerational wealth and security.*

This kind of money-first thinking would have made perfect sense to me back when I was working overtime and chasing bonuses. But Richards was rightfully incensed by his friend's judgment, because he understands the riches to be found in connecting with his family. After all, the happiest times in our lives are not spent in the pursuit of money—rather, it is in the pursuit of emotional wealth.

"The most financially insecure people I know are the ones with the most money," he said. "But security's a myth. My twenty-three-year-old wants to go to medical school, and I don't know how we'll pay for it. But I'm totally okay with that. I've gotten comfortable with living in a spot where I don't have financial certainty. And I am always going to go take a vacation with her in Baja, even when I should probably take a speaking engagement instead."

As you seek out your own sense of enoughness, remember that it often lives at the intersection of financial health and emotional wealth. This place of MoneyZen is where you are able to meet your core financial needs while also seeking out the experiences and connections that bring you joy—that's the place where life feels the most meaningful and balanced. And the coordinates of your place of enoughness can change as your life's circumstances change. That's what happened to my dear friend Mary LoVerde.

LoVerde is a bestselling author and life-balance strategist who spent the first part of her career, from 1977 to 1994, as the director of the Hypertension Research Center at the University of Colorado School of Medicine. Back then, the prevailing lifestyle among patients who sought hypertension treatment at the center was "go as fast as you can, don't sleep, make fifty meals on the weekend, and exercise at three in the morning," LoVerde told me with a wry smile. She began to notice small behavioral distinctions between people, like her patients, who lived in a constant state of overdrive versus the healthy thriving people in her life.

"The healthy people seemed to have time to talk with me. They looked me in the eye. They did not give me a litany of their problems, or all the things they needed to get done," she recalled. Eventually, she identified a single distinguishing factor between this thriving population and people who were constantly scrambling to keep up and get ahead: Connection.

"They did not ask the question, 'What do I need to do?' Because that's a very long, very overwhelming list that nobody will get done," LoVerde explained. "What they asked instead was, 'With whom or what should I connect?'"

Connection creates balance. That was the answer her research found time and again. "Connection with yourself, with your family, your friends, your colleagues, your community, your god. If you feel overwhelmed, look at something on that list," she said.

This discovery was so simple, yet so profound, that it would change LoVerde's life forever. Eventually she left the world of hypertension and cardiac disease and went on to have an incredibly successful career as an author, Fortune 500 speaker, and four-time guest on *Oprah*, inspiring millions of people to get off the time-management hamster wheel and instead focus on connection.

But at age fifty-seven, LoVerde started to feel a lack of connection in her own life. Something was missing. Her sense of "enough" had changed.

"It was one of those light switches," she said. "I lived in Denver, but I had gone to Hawaii to write. I was working on another book. When I came back home and I walked into my beautiful dream home and I looked around, it was gorgeous and I had decorated it within an inch of its life, but a very calm, clear voice said to me, 'All the reasons that you needed and wanted this house are complete. Go.'"

Not one to be pushed around, however, LoVerde argued against that voice in her head.

"I was single, my kids were gone, and this was my nirvana. I had this house exactly the way I wanted. It was Zen-like, and I was never leaving. Never," she recalled.

But the voice argued back. "It said, 'It's not too big, too lonely, too expensive. It's not too anything. There's nothing wrong with it. It's complete,'" she said. "I realized that I was still living as if I was a dog with an electric fence, only nobody told me the fence had been turned off."

In other words: She had raised her family in this wonderful home, but its purpose had been fulfilled. Not only did she not need this house anymore, it had become a financial tether that was keeping her from experiencing greater emotional wealth. It was time to slip out of the tether.

With freedom calling her to roam, LoVerde sold her house in 2010, had a big party, and gave away all her belongings—the artwork, furniture, silverware, everything. The day she left her dream home, LoVerde went into each room to thank it for the memories and love she experienced. "Then I got to the front door and sobbed so hard I thought I'd lose a lung," she said. "But that proverbial peace comes over you and you know you're taking the right steps."

She closed the door and headed out. For the next three years, LoVerde traveled the world, without a home or a plan. She called it her make-it-up-as-you-go global adventure.

"I thought, 'Okay, what do I value and what are my policies about those values?' and I decided one of my policies was: I'm not going to take the trip, the trip is going to take me," she said. "I had to really teach myself to trust that whatever I need, whenever I needed it, for as long as I needed, it will always be at hand. I recited that phrase every day."

Reflecting on her experience, and the big leap she took to start it, LoVerde noted that the key for anyone who is considering a major reset in their life is to get very clear about what makes *you* feel good. Put another way: What will bring you a greater sense of enoughness?

"It's not just about giving it all up and doing something different. It's connecting with yourself about what it is you want," she says. "Maybe what you really want is a house with a yard. You've been living in an apartment the whole time, but what you've always longed for is a garden. The direction that you go in is: *Do I feel good? What will make me* really *feel good?*"

For LoVerde, indulging those stirrings of wanderlust was the answer to what felt good to her at age fifty-seven. But then, after three years on the road, she changed course again. While visiting with her daughter in Denver, she met an enchanting local whom she began to call "Mr. Right."

After about ten months of dating, Mr. Right declared his love for Lo-Verde and asked her to move in. As much as she enjoyed her freedom to roam, she loved this man even more. Without him, the road was no longer enough for LoVerde.

"I'm ever the richer for having had that experience," she said. "I know I can live with next to nothing, and I also know that I can enjoy each and every beautiful thing I own."

LoVerde's story reminds us that when you tether yourself to ideas that no longer serve you, you slowly blunt your instinct to wander and discover joy—to seek out greater emotional wealth. To find your enough.

By definition, emotional wealth comes from connection. Or as Lo-Verde puts it, "Connection creates balance." So, when you are out of balance—when you're in that place where you feel as if there's never enough time or money or joy in your life—ask yourself: *To whom or what do I need to connect?*

Despite her many professional accomplishments, LoVerde can easily pivot toward her own place of MoneyZen. She knows innately what *enough* looks like when it comes to both her financial health and her emotional wealth.

But for those of us who have spent a lifetime fighting the Hungry Ghost, chasing after work, money, and prestige—we often need a little more help defining enoughness when it comes to our financial health. That's where Georgia Lee Hussey comes in.

Hussey is a certified financial planner and the founder and CEO of Modernist Financial, a Portland, Oregon–based wealth management firm that specializes in helping progressive-minded investors grow their money according to their deepest values.

When clients first approach her, they often bring concerns along the lines of " 'Can you help me navigate the world of capitalism and wealth responsibly without feeling like I'm selling my soul?' " Hussey says. "And that's really where the question comes in: How can they stand in their authentic integrity? Not their parents', not their grandparents', not their neighbors' or their business groups'—but their authentic integrity in terms of the way they navigate their business life, their financial life, their investing life."

Hussey and her team developed a company manifesto to help them do just this, and within that document are these guiding words:

"Believe in plenty. Believe in enough."

It's a sentiment that resonates for her clients, many of whom have taken it on as their own personal mantra, posting it on their office bulletin boards. (I have it on mine, too.) Hussey believes in this motto so much, she had it registered as a trademark. As she explained when we spoke recently, the inspiration behind these words began as a personal examination of her own money habits.

"I was trying to get deeper and ask, 'What is the core difficulty that I experience with clients and in myself?' And really it is believing in enough, paired with actually understanding what plenty would be," she said. "If I'm in any financial situation or life situation involving resources, believing in 'enough' is a very important thought practice, because I need to actually know: What would I be satisfied with? When I'm able to take a little bit of space to reflect on what plenty and enough mean for me, I just show up with much more integrity and kindness and clarity."

The idea that a fellow financial services professional would encourage clients to believe there is enough, maybe even *plenty*, was so foreign to me and my Wall Street DNA that it took a while to appreciate this motto. But when I experimented using it as a mental chant, it set my mind at ease and slowed my pulse whenever toxic thoughts around money, work, and prestige came up. As Hussey explained, going from "Never Enough" to "Believe in Plenty" isn't easy, and it takes practice.

"I think, for me, 'enough' comes in the moments of gratitude," she said. "It's that sense of, 'It's been a hard day, but I'm very grateful for shelter, food, and love.' Just boiling it down to the basic needs that I'm so grateful to have that so many people around me don't have. 'Enough' and 'plenty' require a practice of reflection and gratitude when life feels urgent and lacking in resources."

This kind of big-picture awareness speaks volumes about Hussey's own path toward the liberation of enough. Growing up in Ohio in a family that often lacked resources—and did their best to hide that fact—Hussey was keenly aware of the fraught role money played in her life.

"I had a ton of class privilege. I was taught to be able to navigate in upper-class environments comfortably. And yet there was very little money," she said. "We went consignment-store shopping, and I learned how to buy high-quality fabrics at seventy percent off so that I could be in the world as a person who had money when there really wasn't much."

When Hussey set off on her own, rather than coveting money like many around her had, she rebelled against it. By her twenties, she was a sculptor, performance artist, and writer in New York, living the life of a self-described "little, queer punk, 'business is evil, money is awful'" type. But soon her thinking evolved. She began to see money as a tool to problem-solve social issues that she truly cared about.

"I think business is actually a super-radical place to be political and to be able to make real commitments toward doing well for the world around us," Hussey said. She founded Modernist Financial in 2015; in 2017 it was one of the earliest financial advisory firms to become certified as a B Corp, a designation awarded to "businesses that meet the highest standards of verified social and environmental performance, public transparency, and legal accountability to balance profit and purpose," according to B Lab, the nonprofit entity behind B Corp.

"B Corp was one way to hold myself accountable, as a business owner, to doing business in a way that is good for more than just myself," Hussey explained. The B Corp guidelines act as a guard against a common problem she has seen time and again in her own life and among her clients: When we operate from a place of Never Enough, it can lead us to feelings of envy and greed.

"Greed to me is one of the great poisons in our life," she said. "When we hoard or pull in too much for ourselves, it's not a healthy, vibrant place to live."

In line with this thinking, Hussey often makes tough asks of clients, challenging the conventional wisdom around money. Questions like *If you believe in enough, do you really need to hammer down your tax rate as low as possible?*

"That's a very specific example of the conversations we're having with clients," she said. "Another thing we've been doing over the past year is, when people are selling assets in their real estate or making a securities transaction or selling a business, whatever it might be, we're recommending that folks consider making a three percent donation for reparations. That is a direct question of 'What is enough, do you really need all that money?' It has been so interesting because everybody we've asked, so far, has said emphatically with their whole hearts, 'No, I don't. And I would love to make a three percent donation for reparations.'"

Being generous in ways that align with their values is often a cathartic experience for clients, Hussey said. Especially when so many have spent years adhering to ideas around money and business that focus exclusively on growth and profits—a recipe for success that comes at a high cost.

"There's a very strong cultural belief in capitalism, that if you're not growing at 10X, you're not successful," Hussey said. "But what happened to the old-fashioned family business that just goes on generation after generation? It doesn't make piles of money, but it produces a good, solid income. I think that's where I see a lot of internal conflict with people, especially my female business owners. They are attaching to the dominant narrative that growth is the most important thing. But they also have a core understanding that they're not going to be able to be a great partner, a great parent, a great business owner all at the same time *and* grow at 10X.

"This idea is also really problematic for them when it comes to selling their community-based business," she continued. "How do you sell for the most? You sell to a venture firm, you sell to a private equity firm.

Now what have you done? You've just basically undermined your core relationship with your employees whom you've loved and cared for all these years. You sell them and their futures to people who do not hold the same values that you do. I mean, every client of mine who sells their company is full of heartache. The only person I've ever worked with who's been happy with selling their company is the one person who sold it to their employees. Everybody else feels like they have undermined their core beliefs for money—something that, generally, they needed *some*, but they usually don't need as much money as they get."

To be clear, growing a successful business is a tremendous feat; generating wealth is a good thing. But when it comes to growing and generating a full, meaningful life, so many of us have lost the thread. Instead of stopping to ask, *What does enough look like for me?* or *How can I use money to create connection?* we hurtle toward the Grow-Sell-Get-Rich slipstream, then do it all over again with a new venture, never pausing to reflect on why we still feel empty and unfulfilled.

"I think that the business world doesn't want us to be reflective," Hussey said. "We have this belief that there's just never enough. And so the financial-defining piece becomes really valuable for people—defining literally how much is enough for *you*?"

Hussey's ideas around financial health may seem radical, yet she's inarguably touched a nerve in the culture. *Goop*, *Vogue*, the *New York Times*, CNBC, *Forbes*, and countless podcasts have interviewed her about her money philosophy because she is successfully tapping into an evolving worldview about the power of wealth to change our lives, better our communities, and bring balance to a world in which too many people are genuinely suffering from a lack of access and resources.

Again, if you have the privilege of meeting your basic needs—that is, if you have enough, and maybe even plenty—then money can be a powerful tool for seeking out human connection and greater emotional wealth. But money cannot do this all-important job if you're hoarding it, using it for retail therapy, or chasing more of it in the hopes it will make you feel whole.

In fact, the further we get from the mindset that money is *the* measure of our happiness and self-worth, the more our definition of "enough" slowly shifts away from financial metrics.

Let's remember Carl Richards's observation that enoughness has nothing to do with money. If we accept this premise, then what do we use to gauge our sense of enough?

This is the question I asked April Rinne, whose book, *Flux: 8 Superpowers for Thriving in Constant Change*, devotes an entire chapter to helping readers "Know Your Enough," which means both defining what is enough for you and recognizing that you are enough.

A big-picture thinker, ranked among *Forbes*'s "50 Leading Female Futurists" of 2020, and an advisor to global organizations on the future of commerce, community, and culture, Rinne has an answer to how we can measure enoughness that is both surprising and poignant: Enough is not about money or possessions; it's about how we move in the world.

"On the whole, humans today are overindexed on stuff and underindexed on humanity—and when I say humanity, I mean human connection, relationships, the feelings of care for one another," Rinne says. "Love, dignity, integrity, trust, respect, compassion, tolerance—these are the things we can never have enough of. And they cost us nothing."

Connection creates balance, as LoVerde says. And after talking to Rinne, I think it's even more than that—connection is a superpower. Connection is the antidote to an obsession with money. When culture, capitalism, and even our own chemistry compel us to be more, do more, have more—we will spend our precious time in pursuit of work, money, and prestige at the cost of connection. As Rinne says, the things that we *really* need more of in order to feel balanced and content—they cost us nothing.

"When we have a life that is full of love, full of people who inspire us, who have time to talk, to have a conversation. When we have time to sleep, to eat well—the simple but important and meaningful things, right? All of a sudden, you realize you don't need to buy a bunch of stuff. You start feeling quite full. Quite content," she said.

Rinne's simple advice for healing a Never Enough mindset? Instead of always chasing after more, consider doing with *less*.

"When we live in a culture of more, the assumption is 'I am unhappy. How do I get happy? I need to add something to my life—to do more or buy more,'" Rinne said.

This assertion is supported by science. In his 2021 book, *Subtract*, author and professor Leidy Klotz describes how he and his team at the University of Virginia conducted tens of thousands of hours of research to find that humans will automatically and consistently default to additive solutions to problems, rather than considering subtractive ideas that are more effective. Klotz argues that subtraction feels so counterintuitive to us that we have trouble subtracting in our homes (Do the kids really need a thousand Legos? Is anyone ever going to sit on that exercise bike again?); at the office (Must we sign on to yet another group-chat, email-management, productivity-boosting application?); and in our institutions (as with overregulation that makes it nearly impossible to build affordable housing or remove structures that have become eyesores).

Rinne has also noticed this phenomenon on an individual level, when it comes to how we approach daily life. As she told me, "We never think, 'Wait a minute. Maybe part of the reason I'm unhappy is because I've got too much already going on. Maybe I could simplify and spend more time on the things that I really love and enjoy.'"

In her book, she offers practical, easy-to-begin practices of subtraction. These include things like removing an app from your phone; canceling one subscription; selling the exercise equipment you haven't used in a decade; letting go of feeling guilty about an obligation; gently ending a negative relationship.

Subtract to find your enough, Rinne says, and it will give you the time and space to discover what really matters to you: "Becoming your best self means stripping back the layers of who you're not, to getting to who you really are."

For workaholics, subtraction can also mean winnowing your to-do list. Recently I taught a course at the Omega Institute, on a rustic 250-acre campus in Rhinebeck, New York. I've been teaching at the Omega retreat for seven years and, in the past, I'd have finished my class on a Friday night and hopped on the first red-eye home so I could quickly move on to the next work project. But now I like to stick around a while. During my most recent stay, I allowed myself to roam untethered for a few days after finishing my classes.

What happened? I got multiple nights of restorative sleep; I explored the beautiful grounds; I reconnected with people I truly admire and enjoy talking with; I got the time to be still and appreciate this incredible opportunity to teach and help people.

What did I lose by subtracting a few days of work? The experience of feeling miserable, exhausted, and overwhelmed. Instead, I felt a deeply contented sense of enoughness.

o o o

Here's the answer to how to define your enough: It's what *you* decide it to be. There is no single magic number, or letters after your name, or level of career achievement that will give you a feeling of enoughness. Your definition will be unique to your life experiences, family needs, and comfort levels.

For some, enough means you live in a modest city apartment with very few belongings. For others, a house in the suburbs, with a pool and a Ping-Pong table where all the kids like to play after school—that's their idea of enough. You might even decide that a sense of enough isn't about stuff at all—it's about whether you have enough love, delight, adventure, and wonder in your life. It's really up to you.

My own journey has involved lots of false starts, so I know how hard it can be to break negative habits around money-obsession. To help, I've created a few simple tools that keep money's true purpose front of mind.

These tools are like a gut check on conventional ideas around money that may not align with what your heart wants. But you can be flexible about how you use them, so that they don't become yet another to-do assignment or competitive race toward the gold. In fact, the four tools I'm going to share with you are based on a concept that I call Joy-Based Spending.

JOY-BASED SPENDING

For a good part of my life, despite being surrounded by the vast wealth of my peers, I was a die-hard *under*spender. I can recall a time in my midthirties, on a date at the movies, when the man I was with asked if I wanted popcorn or a soda. Back then, all I could think was, *Wait, you actually buy that stuff at the theater?*

Money so defined my sense of self-worth that I was determined to hold on to every penny. And frankly, lots of people are in the same boat I was in: We have enough disposable income to enjoy an indulgence now and then, yet we will still brew every cup of coffee at home, clip coupons like it's our job, and fearfully hold on to each dollar because of toxic emotions around money that make spending an incredibly frightful experience.

It doesn't help that financial gurus and media pundits love to chide us for our $7 lattes, or for taking a $20 cab ride instead of public transportation, or for having a gym membership. Thousands of dollars a year, *wasted*, we're told by the experts. But I'm not so sure.

Like I mentioned in Chapter 5, one of the greatest small pleasures in my life is lingering over a good book in a buzzy coffeehouse. If I pay $5 for a mug of pour-over coffee and I stay there for three hours, I'm getting extreme joy for less than $2 an hour. Likewise, the person who spends $20 on an air-conditioned cab, instead of squeezing onto a crowded subway, might feel joy in knowing they'll arrive refreshed, confident, and ready for a make-or-break meeting. The person who spends five nights a week at the gym, blowing off steam and clearing their mind before they head home to their family, knows that working out gives them the kind

of physical endurance and mental presence they need to be a good parent
and partner.

The point is, for far too long, we've relied on experts and trends to
tell us how to think about and use our money. But only you know what is
wasteful spending and what is worth every penny to you. The key is being
curious and observant about the effects different uses of money have on
your personal happiness meter.

For example, researchers have found that for many people, some of
the most meaningful purchases are ones made in the pursuit of human
connection. (There's that word again!) According to a longitudinal study
of one thousand Harvard students, the happiest graduates a year out of
school were those who had reported that they valued time over money.
Further, the students who spent more time with friends and engaging in
hobbies had greater levels of happiness than those who spent their spare
time working extra hours. In this context, that sixty-inch high-definition
TV around which you gather with friends to watch the latest episode of
Bridgerton may be a scientifically proven *optimal* use of money, if it's in
the service of greater human connection.

So rather than approaching expenses from a deficit model, what would
happen if we flipped everything 180 degrees and operated from a joy
model? When you're trying to decide, like Ani from Chapter 6, whether
to buy the organic tomatoes or the cheaper nonorganic ones, rather than
calculating the extra cost you'll incur, what if instead you calculated the
additional pleasure this purchase might bring? This is where the concept
of Joy-Based Spending comes in.

Joy-Based Spending is the opposite of budgeting. It's a concept I came
up with after seeing time and again that the mere mention of the "B"
word (budget) to clients and students caused their eyes to glaze over and
their ears to shut down. I had to figure out a way to make budgeting fun.
When I started thinking about the role it played in my own life, I realized
that I was so excessively frugal that spending money had become devoid
of all joy. I was very diligent at tracking it, but I didn't connect the dots
between how I spent money and the level of joy I was experiencing in life.

Joy-Based Spending gave me that context. I first tested it on myself and have now been teaching it widely for over a decade.

At its core, Joy-Based Spending is about squeezing the maximum amount of pleasure out of each dollar you spend, so that your financial values are aligned with your emotional values—whether that's connection, creativity, authenticity, nature, or whatever realms you reflected on in Chapter 6.

Joy-Based Spending isn't about rules or limits; it's about shifting your thinking about how to use money. As with anything, reimagining the role money plays in our lives takes practice. Below, I've listed the three tools that I use for myself and recommend to others, as a means to get into the swing of a Joy-Based Spending practice. These tools are based on mindful-money practices that have been around for decades, and they are certainly not the only way to achieve financial health and/or emotional wealth. They simply provide an easy way to remind us of the job money is intended for. If you develop Joy-Based Spending practices you'd like to share with others, I'd love to hear about them. Reach out to me at MoneyZen.com and we can spread the word!

TOOL 1. DO A JOY AUDIT

Here's how I do this: Take out a notebook and write down everything you spend money on, rounded to the nearest dollar. Make sure to include expenses you automatically pay for, like cell phone bills, music memberships, and any cloud-based tech services. Don't forget to jot down things you've prepaid, like camp for the kids or a down payment on a summer vacation. If you can record your expenditures for a month, that's fantastic. You'll have a lot to work with. But even if you can only record a week's worth of expenses, you'll still get a helpful snapshot.

When you're done, here's the best part: You don't have to add anything up. Just take out a yellow highlighter and highlight anything on your list that *does not bring you joy*. For most people, the obvious ones are utility bills, auto repairs, medical fees. Are any of these costs negotiable?

Can you call your cable provider and ask for a lower rate, or drop channels and services you don't use? (Keep the ones that bring you entertainment and joy, of course.)

The more interesting line items will be nuanced expenses, like sports or music lessons. The kids hate the soccer coach, and you don't enjoy driving to practice and games three times a week. So *why* are you dragging everyone through this unpleasant exercise? On the other hand, sometimes these expenses provide delayed joy: Your kids complain about music lessons, and they are *so* expensive; but you believe to your core that learning music is good for their brains, and, in the long run, it will be a delight for them to pick up their instrument anywhere in the world and let music flow from their fingers.

As you go through your list, it may help to remember that while we live in a society that loves instant gratification, joy doesn't always happen immediately. It often comes slowly, with practice and presence of mind.

Tool 2. Do an Hourly Wage Test

One of the most valuable lessons I took away from Vicki Robin and Joe Dominguez's book *Your Money or Your Life* is the reminder that money is obtained through the time we spend working; therefore when we spend it, we're spending our life's energy. Unfortunately, it has become too easy to mindlessly spend this precious energy, fast, without thinking about how our purchases make us feel. That's why the hourly wage test is one of my favorite tools to use when I'm torn about whether or not to buy something.

We all know that we tend to spend more when we use plastic versus cash. But we've also seen how using preprogrammed log-ins at shopping sites, and one-click purchasing so that our credit card numbers instantly populate, leads us into seamless spending that feels effortless—until the credit card bill comes. The result is that we often experience a disconnect between what we spend money on and what our soul wants.

So how can we optimize the spending of our life's energy? Do an hourly wage test.

Theoretically, most of us spend about 2,000 hours a year in work-oriented activities. For this exercise, take your annual gross income and divide it by 2,000. Let's say you're making $60,000 a year. Divided by 2,000, that's about $30 an hour before taxes. Now you can use this figure to stress-test spending choices. For example, when you look at your joy audit, you see that you're paying the dog walker $300 a month (or about 10 hours of your life's energy). You might think to yourself: *I spend almost an entire waking day of my life's energy for someone else to walk Max? I'd actually like to walk the dog more often . . .*

Another example: You're shopping for a new smartphone, and you see one that you *really* want. You think: *Okay, at $999, that's 33 hours of life energy. Is it worth it to me?* The answer very well may be yes. But you now have a personal measuring stick with which to make that decision.

Often, when you equate the item you want with the amount of work it will take to buy it, you can discern pretty quickly whether or not a big expense is worth it, because A) the hourly wage test slows you down, allowing you to be more mindful in a fast-paced world that encourages rapid spending; and B) it forces you to think about the item in terms of both the joy *and* the pain it brings.

You certainly know the pain I'm talking about if you've ever gone out to dinner with friends, everyone orders cocktails, somebody chooses a bottle of wine, then another, and when the bill comes you all split the check. That's the moment when you may be thinking: *Wow, was that experience worth almost a full day of work? Maybe what I value is not totally aligned with this kind of expense. Next time, I'm going to order in pizza and beer and invite everyone over to my place!*

TOOL 3. TAKE A PHOTO

Last but not least, snapping a picture and letting the item simmer in my mind is something I do all the time when I'm weighing an impulse purchase: *This dress would be perfect for the company holiday party, but will I ever wear it again?* Maybe yes, maybe no. But a photograph creates a magical sort of mindfulness and brings you to a different energetic place from which to judge, rather than thinking about how much work it will cost you—a formula that doesn't resonate with everyone. (If you are shopping online, leaving the item in your digital cart is one way to take a virtual photo.)

Or maybe you're stressed-out and want a day at the spa, but . . . getting the massage and the facial and the mani-pedi, that's pretty expensive. Maybe I could do just one or two services. Let me take a picture on my computer screen of the price list, sit with it, see how it feels. You already have the mathematical knowledge with your hourly wage test of how much life energy this will cost you, but now you're also getting the gut check—you're tapping into both your financial health and emotional wealth.

At times you may find that you've applied the three tools and you're still unsure. That's totally normal. Joy-Based Spending isn't about reaching absolute certainty. It's about discerning between your wants versus needs, and then asking, as LoVerde reminds us, *What will make me* really *feel good?*

Here are some additional questions to reflect on as you employ the three tools:

- When you examine the items on your audit that don't bring you joy, how much of your life's energy in hours do they cost you? Does knowing this impact how you approach these expenses?
- Are there any joyless expenses you can drop? What would you gain (or lose) by cutting them out?
- The next time you confront an impulse buy, take a picture of the item. Sit with it for a few days. When you look at the image again, do you still want it? What does your gut tell you?

As you practice Joy-Based Spending, you'll notice a slow, steady shift in your relationship with money, because your larger goal is no longer about accruing dollars and cents, but about employing it for greater emotional wealth.

"Buy few, but buy best," for example, was a sentiment instilled in me by my grandfather, Bhaskerao Thakor, who grew up quite poor in Gujarat, India. My *dadaji*—Indian for grandpa—understood the value of a rupee. Dadaji's point to me was: If you buy just one high-quality set of bedsheets that you absolutely love to sleep on rather than several cheaper sets that are kind of meh, the quality set will serve you for years to come, and you'll spend less money in the long run by not having to replace them after a few years. But even more importantly, you'll feel great joy every time you get into bed. In other words, the ratio of joy per dollar (or rupee!) will often be greatest if you follow this paradigm.

Speaking of sustainability, you'll also start to "connect the dots" on your purchases, instead of "collect the dots." By that I mean, you'll acquire things that last far beyond the next season or upgrade. When I got divorced, I took very few material possessions with me. In many ways, I was starting with a blank slate. I had no bed, no furniture, no dishes, no towels. When it came to purchasing, say, a sofa and chairs for my new living room, I bought the best I could afford. All these years later, they have held up so well they still look brand-new. And I experience such joy every time I sink into them for a Netflix binge, indulge in my guilty pleasure of reading the latest gossip about the British royal family online, or have a girlfriend over for a cozy catch-up chat.

Instead of seeking out the big purchases/big thrills (think: a flashier, more expensive car, which also comes with bigger insurance premiums and repair bills), perhaps you'll find yourself luxuriating in the micro-blisses and micro-adventures you can achieve from small things—like enjoying a cold beer and people-watching from your apartment stoop on a hot summer evening; handwriting a letter to a friend on pretty stationery, just to say thanks for her good advice; or flying the trick kite that got your family on the beach together on that gorgeous fall day. As Rinne says, the things we truly can't get enough of, like love, connection, trust, compassion—they cost us nothing.

Think about a time when you experienced pleasure in something that cost next to nothing. How can you get more of those micro-blisses in your life? How can you begin to move toward the elements of life that bring you greater emotional wealth?

o o o

As difficult as it was to face a divorce, two medical crises, and leaving a wonderful job before the age of fifty so I wouldn't sabotage my own health again, I am finally on the path toward a more meaningful, more "rich" life. It was a difficult journey, as I was *stubbornly* entrenched in the Cult of Never Enough. But I can see now that transcendence is possible for anyone who seeks it. There is so much life to discover beyond work, money, and accomplishments.

Of course, I still "work." Now, in the second act of my professional life, I've joined a corporate board as an independent mutual fund director and do occasional keynote speaking and consulting. But only Monday through Thursday, which is a privilege I paid for with nearly my entire life's energy. My mental focus has finally shifted. Whether it's swimming laps, doing yoga, playing piano, taking Spanish classes, or planning my next trip to explore a new country and culture, my days are so much richer now than at any other time in my life.

There's a Thomas Wolfe quote Jay shared with me recently that beautifully sums up the change in my thinking: "You have reached the pinnacle of success as soon as you become uninterested in money, compliments, or publicity."

This deliciously logical quote resonates across generations. Philosophers and sages have long counseled that when you feel sad or helpless, the antidote is to connect, to give to others—to look outward. You'll know that your own measure of success is heading in the direction Wolfe espouses, when it becomes less about work, money, and prestige (all inward-focused pursuits), and more about: *When can I get more time with my family? How soon can I get back to spending time playing in nature or reading a book? How can I use my expertise—or my time and resources in general—to help better the lives of the people in my local community who are in need?*

Of course, there will be setbacks. For example, there are times when I overextend myself and just want to crawl into bed and collapse. But in my conversations with LoVerde, Hussey, and Rinne, they all spoke independently about the value of being gentle with yourself as you start to heal from a lifetime of existing in a constant state of Never Enough.

"One of the ways that we suffer less," Hussey said, "is by admitting that we suffer and holding that with kindness and compassion and not feeling like we have to change it."

I've been surprised to discover that in admitting my struggles with the Hungry Ghost, and this pervasive feeling of Never Enough, I've found that I'm not nearly as alone in my experiences as I used to believe. Multitudes of fellow travelers have shared their own challenges with a do-it-all mindset. Together we've inspired each other to inch closer to liberation.

"We're surrounded by cultural messages that tell us: You'll never have enough, do enough, earn enough, accomplish enough," Rinne told me recently. "And all of those get wrapped up into 'you will never be enough.' But every one of us has always been enough. From the day we were born, we are enough."

Greater emotional wealth is always there for you, if you choose it. I know, because I've experienced its power. I've felt the liberation of enough. And I recognize now that enoughness has never been out of my reach. It's always been there, inside me, inside all of us, waiting for us to believe.

Permission to Achieve Less

After interviewing scientists, psychologists, economists, work-life experts, workaholics, and regular folks who have a healthy relationship with work and money, I want to make a compelling and counterintuitive argument for anyone who feels like what they do is never enough:

To live a rich, joyful, and connected life, **Achieve Less.**

Just writing those words down, *Achieve Less*, would have made my skin crawl when I was trapped in the Never Enough mindset. But now? It feels so good to say it out loud. My shoulders drop and I feel like I have permission to exhale. Because achieving less doesn't mean just *doing* less. It means letting go of the Flawed Self-worth Anchors that *drive* us to do more, want more, be more. When you decide to achieve less, you are allowing yourself a moment to pause, breathe, and reflect on whether you are seeking something that is real and meaningful, or just striving yourself crazy. As Rinne would say, you are subtracting to find your enough.

What about you? How does it feel when you say these two words to yourself: *Achieve less.*

Is it scary? Ridiculous? Soothing? Rebellious? If it's too much to fathom, like it once felt for me, what if you just said: *Let me try to achieve less today.*

What if you carved out a single twenty-four hours to do . . . nothing of importance. You don't have to accomplish anything. You just get to explore joy. Go easy on yourself. There's no judgment. Whatever the course of your day brings, enjoy how it feels to be liberated from the Cult of Never Enough for twenty-four hours.

I recognize that many people cannot even take one day off, even on weekends, without facing financial challenges. But just as one occasionally needs a sick day to recover from the flu, an "achieve less" mental health day helps us to recover and reset negative Never Enough habits that have turned many of us into prodigious worker bees, buzzing from one hive to the next, making a ton of honey—and never stopping to savor what we've worked so hard to produce. When we view our professions and achievements as the channels through which we pursue self-worth, we forget how to wander, discover, and connect with other people.

Taking a day to achieve less reminds me of something Ani, the yoga instructor, told me when we were commiserating over our Never Enough lifestyles.

"Manisha," she said, "*everyone* I meet is like, 'I'm so busy. I'm so tired.' People don't ever say, 'You know what I did yesterday? I watched three episodes of *Schitt's Creek* and I ate some brownies. Yeah, I didn't really do anything.' I mean, I don't know *anyone* who would say that!"

Nor do I. But the very idea feels exhilarating. The thought of taking a leisurely walk outside, browsing the biography section at the bookstore, and curling up on the couch with a glass of cabernet to listen to a podcast with Jay—that sounds absolutely decadent to me.

That's because I know—we all *innately* know—that taking time for "I am enough" self-care allows you to consciously slow down and be curious about the world around you. You can sit on the grass outside, feel the sun on your face, and clear out the clutter in your mind. Try to be present with how it feels in your bones to just *live*. If it feels really uncomfortable, that's okay. Discomfort is a sign that your brain is struggling with something new. Honor that feeling, then let it go and return your focus to the world around you.

"Achieve less" is a mantra I truly believe in, because I know that when we obsess over achieving more—more money, possessions, prestige, career progression—we lose out on precious opportunities to discover the simple daily pleasures that bring us joy.

There's an apt story that I've heard retold from various cultural perspectives, and here's the version I like to tell: There was a man who made very good *puri*, a type of fried Indian flatbread. One afternoon, an investment banker dropped by the man's street cart to try this puri he'd heard so much about. After a few bites, he turned to the vendor and said: "This is the best puri I've *ever* had. I can't believe you're selling it from a tiny cart."

The vendor shrugged. But the banker saw a great business opportunity unfolding before his eyes. He paced in front of the cart as he pitched his vision: "First, you've got to take out a loan to build a proper industrial kitchen. Your business will grow so big, you'll need to hire a staff of workers and create a distribution network. Then you can buy a factory to produce a thousand times the amount of puri mix you're making now. Soon you'll be selling your puri mix in supermarkets around the world. Then you'll be able to take the company public. Then you'll be so wealthy, you can retire and lie around in a hammock all you want."

The banker turned to get the man's reaction. But the puri maker had retired to a nearby tree and was fast asleep with a smile on his face, swaying in his hammock.

Sometimes, by achieving less, you can focus on the things you really want in the first place: whether that's more time with your family, more freedom to travel, or just an uninterrupted nap in a swaying hammock.

Now that I'm finally free from the Cult of Never Enough, it feels like my world has gone from black and white to color. The tether around my ankle is gone and I have a deep sense of being so much more *alive*. Counterintuitively, letting go of fear, shame, and all the "shoulds" that drove my Never Enough mindset has made me feel . . . safer. And freer than I've ever felt before.

I hope that anyone who finds resonance with any part of my story knows this: You are not alone in your struggles.

If you have ever thought to yourself, *I work so hard, I don't think I can push the gas pedal down any harder, so why am I still . . . unhappy, unfulfilled, alone, afraid, ashamed?* you are simply experiencing the symptoms of a society that's been built on the false belief that the answer to our collective angst is to pursue more work, more money, more prestige. "More" is the fuel of an obsessively materialistic society. But more stuff is not the path to a good life. Until the day comes when our society values happiness over productivity, we must choose to wield our own power over how we live our lives.

We can aspire to *Be* what we love, instead of hewing to the false belief that happiness only exists in doing. We can operate as if we already believe in plenty—no matter what our colleagues, friends, neighbors, family members, or wealthy cousins say that we should or shouldn't be doing when it comes to money, work, and accomplishments. We can gently thank them for their advice, and instead choose to live a balanced life full of financial health and emotional wealth. We can all choose to live in a place of MoneyZen.

o o o

If you'd like to continue the conversation, reach out to me at MoneyZen.com, where you'll also find a *MoneyZen* Book Club Guide, *MoneyZen* Journal, and financial health resources for a wide range of income levels and life experiences. I can't wait to hear from you!

–Manisha

ACKNOWLEDGMENTS

———

Virtually every acknowledgment page of any book I've read starts off with some variation of "It takes a village to write a book." That's because, well, it does. I'd like to thank my amazing literary agent, Lucinda Halpern, along with Ron Friedman and Julia Collucci, for seeing the ways in which a book like this could help so many people long before I had the courage to believe it. And if that isn't enough, they also connected me to the glue that binds this entire book together, the amazing Lisa Sweetingham—a book collaborator and editorial consultant of such exquisite talents, there really are not words to properly express how grateful I am to have had the opportunity to collaborate with her. So I will simply say, Lisa, but for you, this book would never have come to fruition.

One of the interesting things about getting a book into publication is the multiple layers of people who need to believe in and support your project along the way. To that end, I'd like to thank Wendy Wong for seeing the possibilities of this narrative and acquiring this book for Harper Business, along with the incredible support of Hollis Heimbouch, SVP/ publisher of Harper Business, and executive editor of Harper. Thank you to Rachel Kambury, who brought the book across the finish line with her insightful edits; to editorial assistant James Neidhardt, for being such a delight to work with; and to copy editor Tom Pitoniak, for his eagle eyes. A very big thank you also to the marketing and PR teams at Harper Business, especially Amanda Pritzker, Laura Cole, Jessica Gilo, and Leslie Cohen. Last but not least, I'd like to thank Mark Fortier and his team at

Fortier PR, especially Matt Wendler, Elena Christie, Helena Sandlyng, and Brooke Craven for all their hard work.

There were so many incredible individuals who generously shared their personal stories and their professional expertise. My deepest thanks to "Ani," "Priya," "Dominique," "Lauren," and "Jade" for allowing me to share with readers the experiences that cut deep to each of your cores. To Sara McElroy and Jonathan Frostick for putting your personal stories out in the world for us all to learn from. And to our roster of experts: Your research, observations, and insights provided the intellectual backbone to transform this book from an N-of-1 story into a universal framework and thought-provoking process backed by science and verifiable facts: Dr. Belinda Campos, Dr. Malissa Clark, Dr. Eli Cook, Dr. Rebecca Heiss, Georgia Lee Hussey, Kathleen Kingsbury, Dr. Kate Levinson, Dr. Marc Lewis, Mary LoVerde, Helaine Olen, Lindsey Pollak, Carl Richards, April Rinne, Vicki Robin, Dr. Bryan Robinson, and Cali Williams Yost.

Behind the scenes, Mary Cecchini, human Swiss army knife and marketing genius, helped me with everything from rethinking how to make my website and monthly educational newsletter more useful to readers of this book to navigating social media in a way that felt authentic to me—all while she was earning her MBA. Many thanks also to Sabrina Frusco, the wonderful Wellesley College intern who helped get me prepped for the book's prelaunch campaign. And finally, thanks to Michelle Segar for her deep and comprehensive read of the manuscript that helped to level it up.

Of course, without my amazing family there would be no book to write. Through all the ups and downs they have been here to cheer me on in good times and pick me up during the rough patches. Doof and Moof, I love you so much. Suni, Kristin, Captain, Nugget, and Wildman, you make my heart sing. And Jay, you really are the greatest ever.

Finally, I wrote this book for you, dear reader, and the millions of others like us who struggle with a feeling that, no matter what we do, it is Never Enough. Despite our best efforts to thrive, we have found ourselves at times tangled in a toxic web of money, work, prestige, and accomplishments. I'd so love to hear about your own journey toward MoneyZen. Let's continue the conversation on social media. You can find me, all my social links, and valuable financial wellness content for a wide variety of incomes and stages of life at MoneyZen.com.

Notes

Introduction

5 **Simon Sinek asserts**: Simon Sinek, *Start with Why: How Great Leaders Inspire Everyone to Take Action* (New York: Portfolio/Penguin, 2009), 39.

Chapter 1 | Never Enough

17 **money problems and money worries**: I first started thinking about this distinction after reading a book in the School of Life series, specifically John Armstrong, *How to Worry Less about Money* (New York: Macmillan, 2012), 3–4, 9–11.

17 **top 0.1 percent of Americans**: David Leonhart and Yaryna Serkez, "America Will Struggle After Coronavirus. These Charts Show Why," *New York Times*, April 10, 2020, www.nytimes.com/interactive/2020/04/10/opinion/coronavirus-us-economy-inequality.html.

17 **two-thirds of Americans**: Jessica Dickler, "Two-Thirds of Americans Live Paycheck to Paycheck as Inflation Continues to Climb," CNBC, May 11, 2022, www.cnbc.com/2022/05/11/two-thirds-of-americans-live-paycheck-to-paycheck-as-inflation-climbs.html.

18 **Tara Brach describes**: Tara Brach, "De-Conditioning the Hungry Ghosts," *Psychology Today*, September 5, 2017, www.psychologytoday.com/us/blog/finding-true-refuge/201709/de-conditioning-the-hungry-ghosts.

20 **Thich Nhat Hanh reminds**: "Touching Peace: An Evening with Thich Nhat Hanh," YouTube, November 2, 2020, 1:06, youtu.be/g6atIQfEGwc.

20 **karoshi**: "Number of Suicides Related to Problems at Work in Japan from 2012 to 2021," Statista, April 5, 2022, www.statista.com/statistics/622325/japan-work-related-suicides/.

20 **thirty-five employees to commit suicide**: Adam Nossiter, "3 French Executives

Convicted in Suicides of 35 Workers," *New York Times,* Dec 20, 2019, www
.nytimes.com/2019/12/20/world/europe/france-telecom-suicides.html.

20 ***1,600 people in China***: Shai Oster, "In China, 1,600 People Die Every Day
from Working Too Hard," Bloomberg, July 3, 2014, www.bloomberg.com
/news/articles/2014-07-03/in-china-white-collar-workers-are-dying-from
-overwork.

20 ***745,000 deaths***: "Long Working Hours Increasing Deaths from Heart Disease and Stroke: WHO, ILO," World Health Organization, May 17, 2021,
www.who.int/news/item/17-05-2021-long-working-hours-increasing-deaths
-from-heart-disease-and-stroke-who-ilo.

21 ***minister Wayne Oates***: W. E. Oates, *Confessions of a Workaholic: The Facts
About Work Addiction* (New York: World, 1971).

21 ***American Psychological Association's* Dictionary of Psychology**: APA
Dictionary of Psychology, accessed January 13, 2022, dictionary.apa.org
/workaholism. The full definition is: "n. the compulsive need to work and
to do so to an excessive degree. A **workaholic** is one who has trouble re-
fraining from work. This type of driven overinvolvement in work is often a
source of significant stress, interpersonal difficulties, and health problems.
Also called **ergomania**."

21 ***Bergen Work Addiction Scale***: "Driven to Work," University of Bergen,
www.uib.no/en/news/36450/driven-work.

22 ***Malissa Clark***: See more of her work at psychology.uga.edu/directory
/people/malissa-clark.

22 ***found the following common traits***: Malissa A. Clark, "Workaholism: It's
Not Just Long Hours on the Job," Psychological Science Agenda, April
2016, www.apa.org/science/about/psa/2016/04/workaholism.

23 ***four dimensions***: Author interview; see also Malissa Clark, "These Are the
Four Drivers of Workaholism," *Fast Company*, February 20, 2018, www
.fastcompany.com/40531406/there-are-four-types-of-workaholic-and-none
-of-them-work.

24 **psychologically detach *from our jobs***: Lieke ten Brummelhuis and Nancy P.
Rothbard, "How Being a Workaholic Differs from Working Long Hours—
and Why That Matters for Your Health," *Harvard Business Review,*
March 22, 2018, hbr.org/2018/03/how-being-a-workaholic-differs-from
-working-long-hours-and-why-that-matters-for-your-health; and Lieke L.

Ten Brummelhuis, Nancy P. Rothbard, and Benjamin Uhrich, "Beyond Nine to Five: Is Working to Excess Bad for Health?" *Academy of Management Discoveries* 3 (2017): 262–83, journals.aom.org/doi/10.5465/amd.2015.0115.

25 **hedonic treadmill**: Oxford Reference, accessed January 13, 2022, www.oxfordreference.com/view/10.1093/oi/authority.20110803095928134.

26 **Workaholics Anonymous**: "The Twenty Questions," Workaholics Anonymous, accessed November 29, 2022, workaholics-anonymous.org/10-literature/24-twenty-questions.

26 **Jonathan Frostick**: See @Jonathan Frostick LinkedIn post: www.linkedin.com/posts/jonathanfrostick_heartattack-decisionmaking-leadershiplessons-activity-6787207960864014336-sdhA/; Maria Cramer, "After His Heart Attack, a British Man's Rules for Living Take Off on LinkedIn," *New York Times,* April 21, 2021; and "Man's LinkedIn Post About His Heart Attack Goes Viral as He Addresses How We Overwork Ourselves," *People*, April 22, 2021, www.people.com/human-interest/man-linkedin-post-about-heart-attack-goes-viral-addresses-overwork/.

27 **Sara McElroy**: "Workers Are Burnt Out. Can Companies Fix it?" *The Journal*, January 11, 2022, www.wsj.com/podcasts/the-journal/workers-are-burnt-out-can-companies-fix-it/36f4b15b-07f5-4d18-935c-151ddbb423c8.

29 **divorce rates**: Bryan Robinson, "Wedded to Work," *Psychology Today*, October 20, 2020, www.psychologytoday.com/us/blog/the-right-mindset/202010/wedded-work.

30 **"financially contingent self-worth"**: Lora E. Park, Deborah E. Ward, and Kristin Naragon-Gainey, "It's All About the Money (For Some): Consequences of Financially Contingent Self-Worth," *Personality & Social Psychology Bulletin* 43, no. 5 (May 2017): 601–22.

30 **"a desire to achieve"**: D. E. Ward, L. E. Park, C. M. Walsh, K. Naragon-Gainey, E. Paravati, and A. V. Whillans, "For the Love of Money: The Role of Financially Contingent Self-worth in Romantic Relationships," *Journal of Social and Personal Relationships* 38, no. 4 (2021): 1303–28.

30 **In a 2020 paper**: D. Ward, L. E. Park, K. Naragon-Gainey, H. Jung, and A. V. Whillans, "Can't Buy Me Love (or Friendship): Social Consequences of Financially Contingent Self-Worth," *Personality and Social Psychology Bulletin* 46, no. 12 (December 2020): 1665–81.

30 **In a follow-up study**: Ward et al., "For the Love of Money."

Chapter 2 | Shame and Fortune

35 **Diane Fassel**: I first read this in Bryan E. Robinson's *Chained to the Desk*, 3rd ed. (New York: New York University Press, 2014), and the quote is from Diane Fassel and Anne Wilson Schaef, "A Feminist Perspective on Work Addiction," in *Feminist Perspectives on Addictions*, ed. Nan Ven Den Bergh (New York: Springer, 1991), 199–211.

35 **Kathleen Burns Kingsbury**: See more of her work at www.breakingmoney silence.com, and Kathleen Burns Kingsbury, *Breaking Money Silence: How to Shatter Money Taboos, Talk More Openly about Finances, and Live a Richer Life* (Westport, CT: Praeger, 2017).

38 **Per capita income**: It was $303 in 1991 per "India GDP Per Capita 1960–2022," MacroTrends, retrieved March 8, 2022, www.macrotrends.net /countries/IND/india/gdp-per-capita.

42 **childhood traumas**: L. Khoury, Y. L. Tang, B. Bradley, J. F. Cubells, and K. J. Ressler, "Substance Use, Childhood Traumatic Experience, and Post-traumatic Stress Disorder in an Urban Civilian Population," *Depression and Anxiety* 27, no. 12 (2010): 1077–86, doi.org/10.1002/da.20751.

42 **2013 study on survivors**: Z. Chouliara, T. Karatzias, and A. Gullone, "Recovering from Childhood Sexual Abuse: A Theoretical Framework for Practice and Research," *Journal of Psychiatric and Mental Health Nursing* 21, no. 1 (2013): 69–78.

42 **called little-t or small-t traumas**: Elyssa Barbash, "Different Types of Trauma: Small 't' versus Large 'T,'" *Psychology Today*, March 13, 2017, www.psychologytoday.com/us/blog/trauma-and-hope/201703/different -types-trauma-small-t-versus-large-t.

42 **National Institutes of Health**: "How Does Bullying Affect Health and Well-being?" National Institutes of Health, article reviewed on January 31, 2017, www.nichd.nih.gov/health/topics/bullying/conditioninfo/health.

42 **Bryan E. Robinson**: See more of his work at bryanrobinsonbooks.com, and Bryan E. Robinson, *Chained to the Desk in a Hybrid World: A Guide to Work-Life Balance* (New York: New York University Press, 2023).

47 **Extreme perfectionism**: T. Curran and A. P. Hill, "Perfectionism Is Increasing over Time: A Meta-Analysis of Birth Cohort Differences from 1989 to 2016," *Psychological Bulletin* 145, no. 4 (2019): 410–29, www.apa .org/pubs/journals/releases/bul-bul0000138.pdf.

CHAPTER 3 | Striving Ourselves Crazy

58 **Kate Levinson**: Kate Levinson, *Emotional Currency: A Woman's Guide to Building a Healthy Relationship with Money* (Berkeley, CA: Celestial Arts, 2011).

59 **2019 college admissions scandal**: Kate Taylor, "More Parents Plead Guilty in College Admissions Scandal," *New York Times*, October 21, 2019, ny times.com/2019/10/21/us/college-admissions-scandal.html.

60 **could have fed**: Nanci Hellmich, "Cost of Feeding a Family of Four: $146 to $289 a Week," *USA Today*, May 1, 2013, www.usatoday.com/story/news/nation/2013/05/01/grocery-costs-for-family/2104165/.

60 **paid for the annual**: "Average Family Will Spend $800 on Back-to-School," Marketing Charts, July 29, 2011, www.marketingcharts.com/uncatego rized-18563.

61 **"Gross National Happiness Index"**: S. Balasubramanian and P. Cashin, "Gross National Happiness and Macroeconomic Indicators in the Kingdom of Bhutan," IMF Working Papers, 2019 (015), A001, www.elibrary .imf.org/view/journals/001/2019/015/article-A001-en.xml; and "Gross National Happiness Index," UN Sustainable Development Goals, Partnership Platform, retrieved February 28, 2022, sustainabledevelopment.un.org /partnership/?p=2212.

62 **Eli Cook**: Eli Cook, *The Pricing of Progress: Economic Indicators and the Capitalization of American Life* (Cambridge, MA: Harvard University Press, 2017).

64 **halo effect**: A. Sarkar, D. Nithyanand, F. Sella, R. Sarkar, I. Mäkelä, R. Cohen Kadosh, A. J. Elliot, and J. M. Thompson, "Knowledge of Wealth Shapes Social Impressions," *Journal of Experimental Psychology: Applied* 28, no. 1 (2022): 205–36, doi.org/10.1037/xap0000304.

67 **Carl Richards**: See more of his work at behaviorgap.com, and Carl Richards, *The Behavior Gap: Simple Ways to Stop Doing Dumb Things with Money* (New York: Portfolio, 2012).

67 **2021 Experian data**: Chris Horymski, "Consumer Debt Continued to Grow in 2021 Amid Economic Uncertainty," Experian, April 29, 2022, www.experian.com/blogs/ask-experian/research/consumer-debt-study/.

68 **Wall Street Journal *investigation***: Lisa Bannon and Andrea Fuller, "USC

Pushed a $115,000 Online Degree. Graduates Got Low Salaries, Huge Debts," *Wall Street Journal*, November 9, 2021, www.wsj.com/articles/usc -online-social-work-masters-11636435900.

69 **serious financial devastation**: Melissa Hanson, "College Dropout Rates," last updated November 22, 2021, Education Data Initiative, educationdata. org/college-dropout-rates; and Elissa Nadworny and Clare Lombardo, "'I'm Drowning': Those Hit Hardest by Student Loan Debt Never Finished College," NPR, July 18, 2019, www.npr.org/2019/07/18/739451168 /i-m-drowning-those-hit-hardest-by-student-loan-debt-never-finished -college.

70 **median salary**: "How Much Does a Legal Secretary Earn in New York City?" $65,105, Glassdoor, updated February 23, 2022, www.glassdoor .com/Salaries/new-york-city-legal-secretary-salary-SRCH_IL.0,13_IM615 _KO14,29.htm.

71 **would have paid over $19,000**: For tax rates, see Good Calculators, good calculators.com/us-salary-tax-calculator/.

71 **Fictional Financial Lifestyles on TV**: See TV Tropes website for "Friends Rent Control," tvtropes.org/pmwiki/pmwiki.php/Main/FriendsRentCon trol; "Pottery Barn Poor," tvtropes.org/pmwiki/pmwiki.php/Main/Pottery BarnPoor; "Improbable Food Budget," tvtropes.org/pmwiki/pmwiki.php /Main/ImprobableFoodBudget; and "Unlimited Wardrobe," tvtropes.org /pmwiki/pmwiki.php/Main/UnlimitedWardrobe.

72 **divulge the size of their paychecks**: See also Jordan Calhoun, "The One Thing TV Characters Don't Talk About," *Atlantic*, January 7, 2022, news letters.theatlantic.com/humans-being/61d89943a0682f002280a3a8/the -one-thing-tv-characters-dont-talk-about/.

72 **2018 study at the London School of Economics**: See Rodolfo Leyva, "Experimental Insights into the Socio-cognitive Effects of Viewing Materialistic Media Messages on Welfare Support," *Media Psychology*, 2018, eprints .lse.ac.uk/89390/1/Leyva_Experimental_insights_Accepted.pdf; and Stacy Rapacon, "How Your Media-Viewing Habits Impact Your Thoughts About Money," *U.S. News & World Report*, August 20, 2018, money.usnews.com /money/personal-finance/family-finance/articles/2018-08-20/how-your -media-viewing-habits-impact-your-thoughts-about-money.

72 **Allen Ginsberg**: "A Muse Unplugged," editorial, *New York Times*, October 8, 2007, www.nytimes.com/2007/10/08/opinion/08mon4.html.

73 **fifth edition**: "Overuse of Digital Technology May Indicate Addiction, Expert Says," Psychiatric News Alert, American Psychiatric Association, February 9, 2022, alert.psychnews.org/2022/02/overuse-of-digital -technology-may.html. See also *Diagnostic and Statistical Manual of Mental Disorders, Fifth Edition (DSM-5)* (Arlington, VA: American Psychiatric Publishing, 2013).

73 **trigger FOMO**: A. Alutaybi, E. Arden-Close, J. McAlaney, A. Stefanidis, K. Phalp, and R. Ali, "How Can Social Networks Design Trigger Fear of Missing Out?" 2019 IEEE International Conference on Systems, Man and Cybernetics, 2019, pp. 3758–65, doi:10.1109/SMC.2019.8914672; and Giulia Fioravanti, Silvia Casale, Sara Bocci Benucci, Alfonso Prostamo, Andrea Falone, Valdo Ricca, Francesco Rotella, "Fear of Missing Out and Social Networking Sites Use and Abuse: A Meta-analysis," *Computers in Human Behavior* 122 (2021): 106839, doi.org/10.1016/j.chb.2021.106839.

73 **Royal Society for Public Health**: "#StatusOfMind: Social Media and Young People's Mental Health and Wellbeing," Royal Society for Public Health, May 2017, London, www.rsph.org.uk/our-work/campaigns/status -of-mind.html.

74 **Lindsey Pollak**: See more of her work at lindseypollak.com, and Lindsey Pollak, *Recalculating: Navigate Your Career Through the Changing World of Work* (New York: HarperBusiness, 2021).

75 **2018 study from Allianz**: Shawn M. Carter, "Social Media May Be Making You Overspend—and It's Not Just Because of the Ads," CNBC, March 15, 2018, www.cnbc.com/2018/03/15/social-media-may-make-you-overspend -and-its-not-just-because-of-ads.html.

Chapter 4 | ~~Do~~ Be What You Love

78 **the author of this to-do list**: David Streitfeld, "The Epic Rise and Fall of Elizabeth Holmes," *New York Times*, January 3, 2022, www.nytimes .com/2022/01/03/technology/elizabeth-holmes-theranos.html. Her list is referenced in the story at this site: files.cand.uscourts.gov/files/18-CR-258 %20USA%20v.%20Holmes/Trial%20Exh.%207731/Trial%20Exh.%20 7731%20Notes.pdf.

78 **She rubbed elbows**: Noah Kulwin, "Theranos CEO Elizabeth Holmes's Five Best Cover Story Appearances, Ranked," Vox, October 26, 2015, www

.vox.com/2015/10/26/11620036/theranos-ceo-elizabeth-holmess-five-best
-cover-story-appearances.

79 **Tesla CEO Elon Musk tweeted**: His full tweet: "There are way easier places to work, but nobody ever changed the world on 40 hours a week," @elonmusk, Twitter, November 26, 2018, twitter.com/elonmusk/status /1067173497909141504.

79 **Yahoo's former CEO Marissa Mayer claimed**: Max Chafkin, "Yahoo's Marissa Mayer on Selling a Company While Trying to Turn It Around," Bloomberg, August 4, 2016, www.bloomberg.com/features/2016-marissa -mayer-interview-issue/.

79 **Atlantic reporter Derek Thompson**: Derek Thompson, "Workism Is Making Americans Miserable," *Atlantic*, February 24, 2019, www.the atlantic.com/ideas/archive/2019/02/religion-workism-making-americans -miserable/583441/.

80 **"Toil glamour"**: Erin Griffith, "Why Are Young People Pretending to Love Work?" *New York Times*, January 26, 2019, www.nytimes.com/2019/01/26 /business/against-hustle-culture-rise-and-grind-tgim.html.

80 **"struggle porn"**: Nat Eliason, "No More 'Struggle Porn,'" Medium, October 18, 2018, medium.com/@nateliason/no-more-struggle-porn-20215 3a01108.

80 **37 percent of adults under 30**: Kim Parker and Juliana Menasce Horowitz, "Majority of Workers Who Quit a Job in 2021 Cite Low Pay, No Opportunities for Advancement, Feeling Disrespected," Pew Research Center, March 9, 2022, www.pewresearch.org/fact-tank/2022/03/09/majority-of -workers-who-quit-a-job-in-2021-cite-low-pay-no-opportunities-for-advance ment-feeling-disrespected/.

80 **47 percent of respondents**: "Great Expectations: Making Hybrid Work *Work*," Microsoft Work Lab, Work Trend Index Annual Report, March 16, 2022, www.microsoft.com/en-us/worklab/work-trend-index/great-expecta tions-making-hybrid-work-work.

81 **U.S. Treasury secretary Hamilton**: Cook, *The Pricing of Progress*, 43–48.

82 **training a new employee**: Lorri Freifeld, ed., "2021 Training Industry Report," *Training*, November 2021, pubs.royle.com/publication/?m=20617&i =727569&p=20&ver=html5.

82 **pays for lost sleep**: "Lack of Sleep Costing U.S. Economy Up to $411 Billion a Year," RAND press release, November 30, 2016, www.rand.org/news /press/2016/11/30.html.

82 **to age seventeen**: Mark Lino, "The Cost of Raising a Child," U.S. Department of Agriculture blog, February 18, 2020, www.usda.gov/media /blog/2017/01/13/cost-raising-child.

82 **average was $25,230**: "A Child Born in 2011 Will Cost $234,900 to Raise According to USDA Report," U.S. Department of Agriculture press release, June 14, 2012, www.usda.gov/media/press-releases/2012/06/14/child-born -2011-will-cost-234900-raise-according-usda-report.

83 **In 1706, the editor**: See Cook, *The Pricing of Progress*, 97–99, and "The Importation of Negroes into Massachusetts," Learning for Justice, www .learningforjustice.org/classroom-resources/texts/hard-history/the-impor tation-of-negroes-into-massachusetts-1706.

88 **WeWork**: Adam Neumann, "The Beginning of a New Story," WeWork Newsroom, January 8, 2019, www.wework.com/newsroom/wecompany.

88 **journalist Sarah Jaffe**: Sarah Jaffe, *Work Won't Love You Back: How Devotion to Our Jobs Keeps Us Exploited, Exhausted, and Alone* (New York: Bold Type Books, 2021).

89 **Scott Kriens**: "Scott Kriens: Generative Energy—The Real Currency of Life," *True WELLth* podcast, March 27, 2019, www.brightonjones.com/pod cast/scott-kriends/.

90 **4.5 million Americans**: Rory Maurer, "Record 4.5 Million Workers Quit in November," SHRM, January 4, 2022, www.shrm.org/resourcesandtools /hr-topics/talent-acquisition/pages/record-millions-workers-quit-2021-bls -great-resignation.aspx.

90 **low wages and "996" schedules**: James Kynge, "China's Young 'Lie Flat' Instead of Accepting Stress," *Financial Times*, August 2, 2021, www.ft.com /content/ea13fed5-5994-4b82-9001-980d1f1ecc48; and Allen Wan, Amanda Wang, Tom Hancock, Katia Dmitrieva, Carolynn Look, Yuko Takeo, and Samson Ellis, "From the Great Resignation to Lying Flat, Workers Are Opting Out," *Bloomberg Businessweek*, December 2, 2021, www .bloomberg.com/news/features/2021-12-07/why-people-are-quitting-jobs -and-protesting-work-life-from-the-u-s-to-china.

90 *a survey by the IFO Institute*: "More and More Companies Lament Lack of Skilled Workers," IFO Institute, August 12, 2021, www.ifo.de/en/node /64602.

90 *Microsoft study*: "The Next Great Disruption Is Hybrid Work—Are We Ready?" Microsoft Work Lab, Work Trend Index Annual Report, March 22, 2021, www.microsoft.com/en-us/worklab/work-trend-index/hybrid-work.

91 *Bumble gave its employees*: Vicky McKeever, "Dating App Bumble Gives Workers the Week Off to Recover from Burnout," CNBC, June 22, 2021, www.cnbc.com/2021/06/22/dating-app-bumble-gives-workers-the-week -off-to-recover-from-burnout.html.

91 *LinkedIn*: Kathryn Vasel, "To Prevent Burnout, LinkedIn Is Giving Its Entire Company the Week Off," CNN, April 5, 2021, www.cnn.com /2021/04/02/success/linkedin-paid-week-off/index.html/.

91 *Citigroup investment bank instituted*: Jane Fraser, "Latest Update on the Future of Work at Citi," Citigroup blog, March 24, 2021, blog.citigroup .com/2021/03/latest-update-on-the-future-of-work-at-citi/.

91 *Cali Williams Yost*: See more of her work at flexstrategygroup.com/about, and Cali Williams Yost, *Work + Life: Finding the Fit That's Right for You* (New York: Riverhead Books, 2004).

95 *Elizabeth Gilbert*: @elizabeth_gilbert_writer, Instagram, December 29, 2019, www.instagram.com/p/B6qyUR3hfHE/.

96 *Ash Barty's recent announcement*: See Jason Gay, "Introducing Ash Barty . . . as Herself," *Wall Street Journal*, March 23, 2022, www.wsj.com /articles/ash-barty-tennis-retirement-wta-australia-11648049128?st=jtsvlz bzmbcmtgq&reflink=share_mobilewebshare; and @ashbarty, Instagram, March 22, 2022, www.instagram.com/p/Cbbbr7xBX7N/.

CHAPTER 5 | Hardwired to Hustle

100 *a normal sed rate for women*: Mayo Clinic Staff, "Sed Rate, Erythrocyte Sedimentation Rate (ESR)," Mayo Clinic, August 10, 2021, www.mayo clinic.org/tests-procedures/sed-rate/about/pac-20384797.

101 *Severe dengue*: "Dengue and Severe Dengue," World Health Organization, January 20, 2022, www.who.int/news-room/fact-sheets/detail/dengue-and -severe-dengue.

105 **Epstein-Barr**: Nicole Rura, "Epstein-Barr Virus May Be Leading Cause of MS," *Harvard Gazette*, January 13, 2022, news.harvard.edu/gazette/story /2022/01/epstein-barr-virus-may-be-leading-cause-of-multiple-sclerosis/; and "What Is MS," National Multiple Sclerosis Society, retrieved April 25, 2022, www.nationalmssociety.org/What-is-MS.

106 **Rebecca Heiss**: See more of her work at rebeccaheiss.com, and Rebecca Heiss, *Instinct: Rewire Your Brain with Science-Backed Solutions to Increase Productivity and Achieve Success* (New York: Citadel, 2021).

109 **Andrew Huberman describes it**: Huberman in conversation with Dr. Anna Lembke, Huberman Lab podcast, August 16, 2021, at 33:29, hubermanlab .com/dr-anna-lembke-understanding-and-treating-addiction/.

110 **Marc Lewis**: See more of his work at memoirsofanaddictedbrain.com, and Marc Lewis, *The Biology of Desire: Why Addiction Is Not a Disease* (New York: PublicAffairs, 2015).

115 **practice a five-finger piano exercise**: A. Pascual-Leone, D. Nguyet, L. G. Cohen, J. P. Brasil-Neto, A. Cammarota, and M. Hallett, "Modulation of Muscle Responses Evoked by Transcranial Magnetic Stimulation During the Acquisition of New Fine Motor Skills," *Journal of Neurophysiology* 74, no. 3 (September 1995):1037–45, doi:10.1152/jn.1995.74.3.1037; and Sharon Begley, "The Brain: How the Brain Rewires Itself," *Time*, January 19, 2007, content.time.com/time/magazine/article/0,9171,1580438,00.html.

115 **Tiger Woods says**: Matt Chivers, "Tiger Woods Describes Putting Visualization Technique in Classic Footage," GolfMagic, August 15, 2021, www .golfmagic.com/golf-news/tiger-woods-describes-putting-visualisation -technique-classic-footage.

115 **Olympian swimmer Michael Phelps**: "Olympics 2012: Michael Phelps Has Mastered the Psychology of Speed," *Washington Post* YouTube channel, June 5, 2012, www.youtube.com/watch?v=Htw780vHH0o.

116 **science of gratitude**: Linda Roszak Burton, "The Neuroscience of Gratitude," Wharton Health Care Management Alumni Club, University of Pennsylvania, retrieved May 6, 2022, www.whartonhealthcare.org/the_neuro science_of_gratitude. See also Linda Roszak Burton, "Discovering the Health and Wealth Benefits of Gratitude," www.whartonhealthcare.org /discovering_the_health.

116 **25 percent happier moods**: R. A. Emmons and M. E. McCullough,

"Counting Blessings Versus Burdens: An Experimental Investigation of Gratitude and Subjective Well-Being in Daily Life," *Journal of Personality and Social Psychology* 84, no. 2 (2003): 377–89, greatergood.berkeley.edu /pdfs/GratitudePDFs/6Emmons-BlessingsBurdens.pdf; and Anne Morin, "This Daily Habit Will Make You 25 Percent Happier," *Psychology Today*, July 13, 2016, www.psychologytoday.com/us/blog/what-mentally-strong -people-dont-do/201607/daily-habit-will-make-you-25-percent-happier.

CHAPTER 6 | Financial Health + Emotional Wealth = MoneyZen

125 **Vicki Robin**: See more of her work at vickirobin.com, and Vicki Robin and Joe Dominguez, *Your Money or Your Life: 9 Steps to Transforming Your Relationship with Money and Achieving Financial Independence* (New York: Penguin Books, 2018).

131 **human connection is central**: Karynna Okabe-Miyamoto and Sonja Lyubomirsky, "The World Happiness Report 2021, Chap 6: Social Connection and Well-Being during COVID-19," Sustainable Development Solutions Network, Gallup World Poll, March 20, 2021, worldhappiness .report/ed/2021/social-connection-and-well-being-during-covid-19/.

131 **Studies find that loneliness**: See the work of the late John T. Cacioppo, especially his book *Loneliness*, cowritten with William Patrick (New York: Norton, 2008); J. House, K. Landis, and D. Umberson, "Social Relationships and Health," *Science* 241, no. 4865 (1988): 540–45, doi:10.1126/science .3399889; R. Scheffler, T. Brown, L. Syme, I. Kawachi, I. Tolstykh, et al., "Community-Level Social Capital and Recurrence of Acute Coronary Syndrome," *Social Science & Medicine* 66 (2008): 1603–13; and Angus Chen, "Loneliness May Warp Our Genes, And Our Immune Systems," NPR, November 29, 2015, www.npr.org/sections/health-shots /2015/11/29/457255876/loneliness-may-warp-our-genes-and-our-immune -systems.

131 **Harvard Study of Adult Development**: Liz Mineo, "Harvard Study, Almost 80 Years Old, Has Proved That Embracing Community Helps Us Live Longer, and Be Happier," *Harvard Gazette*, April 11, 2017, news.har vard.edu/gazette/story/2017/04/over-nearly-80-years-harvard-study-has -been-showing-how-to-live-a-healthy-and-happy-life/.

132 **Rat Park studies**: B. K. Alexander, B. L. Beyerstein, P. F. Hadaway, and R. B. Coambs, "Effect of Early and Later Colony Housing on Oral In-

gestion of Morphine in Rats," *Pharmacology Biochemistry and Behavior* 15, no. 4 (1981): 571–76, doi:10.1016/0091-3057(81)90211-2; and Bruce K. Alexander, "Rat Park," retrieved May 9, 2022, www.brucekalexander.com /articles-speeches/rat-park/148-addiction-the-view-from-rat-park.

132 **Belinda Campos**: See more of her work at faculty.sites.uci.edu/bcampos/.

132 **for the people who need you**: "What Makes Us Happier Than Money?" The Science of Happiness, Greater Good Science Center, August 20, 2020, YouTube, www.youtube.com/watch?v=foqi_S-6XPo; and B. Campos, I. S. Yim, and D. Busse, "Culture as a Pathway to Maximizing the Stress-Buffering Role of Social Support," *Hispanic Journal of Behavioral Sciences* 40, no. 3 (2018):294–311, journals.sagepub.com/doi/abs/10.1177/0739986318772490.

132 **American military study from 1982**: H. C. Triandis, G. Marin H. Betancourt, J. Lisansky, and B.-H. Chang, "Dimensions of Familism among Hispanic and Mainstream Navy Recruits" (No. TR-ONR-14), 1982, apps.dtic .mil/sti/pdfs/ADA114898.pdf.

135 **Scientific data show that creative endeavors**: Ashley Stahl, "Here's How Creativity Actually Improves Your Health," *Forbes*, July 25, 2018, www .forbes.com/sites/ashleystahl/2018/07/25/heres-how-creativity-actually -improves-your-health/?sh=28c8807013a6; and Tori Rodriguez, "Creativity Predicts a Longer Life," *Scientific American*, September 1, 2012, www.sci entificamerican.com/article/open-mind-longer-life/.

CHAPTER 7 | The Liberation of Enough

140 **elephants in captivity are trained**: This story has taken on mythical qualities, having been retold in motivational speeches, yet there are numerous online sources indicating that the practice takes place around the world. For differing examples, see "Baby Elephants, Bound and Broken: This Is How Circuses Train Elephants," PETA, headlines.peta.org/how-circuses -train-baby-elephants/; "Proper Chain Use," Asian Elephant Support, www .asianelephantsupport.org/uses-for-chains; and "Breaking the Chain That Holds Our Mind—Elephant and Chain," YouTube, www.youtube.com /watch?v=AUBUdewuHUI, all accessed June 30, 2022.

142 **Helaine Olen**: See more of her work at helaineolen.com, and Helaine Olen, *Pound Foolish: Exposing the Dark Side of the Personal Finance Industry* (New York: Portfolio, 2012).

144 **Mary LoVerde**: See "Mary LoVerde: Connection—The Organic Path to Work/Life Harmony," *True Wellth* podcast, April 24, 2019, Episode #8, www.brightonjones.com/podcast/mary-loverde/, and maryloverde.com.

147 **Georgia Lee Hussey**: See more of her work at modernistfinancial.com /georgia-1.

152 **April Rinne**: See more of her work at aprilrinne.com, and April Rinne, *Flux: 8 Superpowers for Thriving in Constant Change* (Oakland, CA: Berrett-Koehler, 2021).

153 **Leidy Klotz**: Leidy Klotz, *Subtract: The Untapped Science of Less* (New York: Flatiron Books, 2021); and G. S. Adams, B. A. Converse, A. H. Hales, et al., "People Systematically Overlook Subtractive Changes," *Nature* 592 (2021): 258–61, doi.org/10.1038/s41586-021-03380-y.

156 **study of one thousand Harvard students**: A. Whillans, L. Macchia, and E. Dunn, "Valuing Time over Money Predicts Happiness after a Major Life Transition: A Preregistered Longitudinal Study of Graduating Students," *Science Advances* 5, no. 9 (September 2019): eaax2615, www.science.org /doi/10.1126/sciadv.aax2615.

162 **Thomas Wolfe**: Though I was unable to find the original source material, this quote is commonly attributed to Wolfe. See, for example, "Thought for the Day," *Los Angeles Times*, May 4, 2010, www.latimes.com /socal/daily-pilot/news/tn-dpt-xpm-2010-05-04-dpt-deboom050510-story .html; and "Thomas Wolfe Quotes," GoodReads, www.goodreads.com /quotes/898914-you-have-reached-the-pinnacle-of-success-as-soon-as.

INDEX

ABOUT THE AUTHOR

MANISHA THAKOR has worked in financial services for more than thirty years, with an emphasis on women's economic empowerment. A nationally recognized thought-leader in this space, Thakor has been featured in a wide range of publications including the *Wall Street Journal*, the *New York Times*, NPR, PBS, CNN, *Real Simple*, and *Women's Health*. Prior to writing *MoneyZen*, Thakor coauthored two personal finance books for women in their twenties and thirties. Today her work focuses on helping women of all ages to balance financial health and emotional wealth. Thakor earned her MBA from Harvard Business School and BA from Wellesley College. She splits her time between Portland, Oregon, and rural Maine. Her website is MoneyZen.com.